Self Help for Men

Confidence, Assertiveness and Self-Esteem Training (3 in 1)

Use These Tools and Methods to Say NO more, to Stop Doubting and to Stop Always Being Mr. Nice Guy

By

John Adams

© **Copyright 2018 - All rights reserved.**

The content contained within this book may not be reproduced, duplicated or transmitted without direct written permission from the author or the publisher.

Under no circumstances will any blame or legal responsibility be held against the publisher, or author, for any damages, reparation, or monetary loss due to the information contained within this book. Either directly or indirectly.

Legal Notice:
This book is copyright protected. This book is only for personal use. You cannot amend, distribute, sell, use, quote or paraphrase any part, or the content within this book, without the consent of the author or publisher.

Disclaimer Notice:
Please note the information contained within this document is for educational and entertainment purposes only. All effort has been executed to present accurate, up to date, and reliable, complete information. No warranties of any kind are declared or implied. Readers acknowledge that the author is not engaging in the rendering of legal, financial, medical or professional advice. The content within this book has been derived from various sources. Please consult a licensed professional before attempting any techniques outlined in this book.

By reading this document, the reader agrees that under no circumstances is the author responsible for any losses, direct or indirect, which are incurred as a result of the use of information contained within this document, including, but not limited to, — errors, omissions, or inaccuracies.

Table Of Contents

PART 1: SELF-ESTEEM FOR MEN	1
CHAPTER 1: INTRODUCTION: WHAT IS SELF-ESTEEM?	2
Is Self-Esteem an Inherent Trait?	3
Loss of Self-Esteem	4
Importance of Self-Esteem	5
CHAPTER 2: THE COMPONENTS OF BUILDING SELF-ESTEEM	9
The Practice of Living Consciously	10
The Practice of Self-Acceptance	11
The Practice of Self-Responsibility	12
The Practice of Self-Assertiveness	14
The Practice of Living with Purpose	16
The Practice of Personal Integrity	18
CHAPTER 3: HABITS AND HOW TO USE THEM FOR GOOD	22
The Cue	23
The Routine	26
The Reward	27
CHAPTER 4: PRACTICAL EXAMPLES	31
The Practice of Living Consciously	31
The Practice of Self-Acceptance	34
The Practice of Self-Responsibility	37
The Practice of Self-Assertiveness	40
The Practice of Living Purposefully	43
The Practice of Personal Integrity	45
CHAPTER 5: WORKBOOK	47
CONCLUSION	59

PART 2: ASSERTIVENESS FOR MEN — 61
CHAPTER 1: INTRODUCTION TO COMMUNICATION STYLES — 62
Passive Communication — 63
Aggressive Communication — 65
Passive-Aggressive Communication — 67
Assertive Communication — 69

CHAPTER 2: WHY DO WE BEHAVE THE WAY WE DO? — 72
Reasons for Aggressive Behavior in Men — 73
Reasons for Passive-Aggressive Behavior in Men — 75

CHAPTER 3: CURRENT LEVEL OF ASSERTIVENESS — 80
Questionnaire #1 to Identify Your Current Level of Assertiveness — 80
Questionnaire #2 to Identify Your Current Level of Assertiveness — 85
Assertiveness Journal to Know Your Current Status — 86

CHAPTER 4: BUILDING ASSERTIVENESS BASED ON YOUR CORE VALUES — 88
Importance of Core Values — 89
Discovering and Defining Core Values — 89
Core Values and Assertiveness — 92

CHAPTER 5: CHANGE YOUR INNER BELIEFS — 95
Assertive Rights — 96
Changing Your Inner Beliefs — 97

CHAPTER 6: COMMUNICATION TECHNIQUES TO PRACTICE — 103
Tips to Improve Assertiveness in Your Communication — 104
Assertive Communication and Handling Criticism — 109
Final Wrap-Up Practice Tips for Assertiveness — 110

CHAPTER 7: TOOLS TO BUILD ASSERTIVENESS — 112
Power Poses to Increase Assertiveness — 114

CHAPTER 8: CONCLUSION — 117

PART 3: CONFIDENCE FOR MEN — 120
CHAPTER 1: INTRODUCTION – UNDERSTANDING CONFIDENCE — 121
- Why is Confidence Important? — 122
- Is Confidence a Genetically Acquired or Learned Skill? — 125
- Confidence and Assertiveness — 127
- Confidence and Self-Esteem — 127
- Cha176
- Chapter Summary — 178
- pter Summary — 128

CHAPTER 2: UNDERSTANDING YOUR CURRENT LEVEL OF CONFIDENCE — 129

CHAPTER 3: HOW TO START BEING CONFIDENT — 138
- Growth Mindset — 138
- Fixed Mindset Triggers and How to Avoid Them — 140
- Learning and Practicing New Skills Until You Master Them — 144
- Chapter Summary — 144

CHAPTER 4: SELF-AWARENESS - KNOW YOUR CORE VALUES — 145
- Importance of Core Values — 146
- Characteristics of Core Values — 147
- Chapter Summary — 152

CHAPTER 5: SETTING GOALS; YOUR MISSION AND PURPOSE — 153
- Why is Goal-Setting Important? — 153
- Chapter Summary — 160

CHAPTER 6: TIPS AND TRICKS TO BUILD CONFIDENCE - PART I — 161
- Building Confidence through Visualizations — 161
- Confidence Building through Affirmations — 163
- Challenge Yourself Continuously — 165
- Journals for Confidence Building — 168
- Chapter Summary — 170

CHAPTER 7: TIPS AND TRICKS TO BUILD CONFIDENCE - PART II	**171**
Avoid Perfectionism	**171**
Love Yourself	**174**
Have a Positive Attitude	
CHAPTER 8: CONCLUSION	**179**

Self Help For Men

Part 1: Self-Esteem for Men

5 Simple But Unused Methods to Start an Inner Journey and Which Will Stop You Being a Doormat

By

John Adams

Chapter 1: Introduction: What is Self-Esteem?

Self-esteem reflects a person's sense of self-worth or self-respect. 'Do you consider yourself a worthy man?' is the question you need to answer to get a basic understanding of your current level of self-esteem. It is a trait that reflects your own opinion about yourself. Other self-beliefs that have a direct effect on the level of self-esteem include:

- Do you think the job you do aligns with your capabilities and qualifications?
- Do you think other people respect you and your profession?
- Do you think your salary and remuneration matches the work you do?
- Do you think your family and friends appreciate you for what you are?
- Do you think your children are proud of having you as their father?
- Do you think you are a good-looking man?
- Do you think you have great social skills?
- Do you believe that you have a good standing in your community and social circle?

Psychologists refer to self-esteem as a personality trait that describes an overall sense of personal value. Therefore, self-esteem can be defined as a measure of how you value and estimate your worth. Unlike other personality traits, such as confidence, which can differ depending on the situation and circumstance, self-esteem tends to endure for a person across all aspects of his life. So, if you have a low level of self-esteem in your personal life, then you probably have similar levels in your professional life as well.

Is Self-Esteem an Inherent Trait?

Typically, self-esteem is an acquired trait that people can learn and master if they put their mind to it. However, genetic factors could play a small role in a person's aptitude for self-esteem. So, if someone has an inherent tendency to be proud of himself, then this person will find it easier to build and develop his self-esteem than someone who is genetically predisposed to be uncertain of himself.

However, it is an irrefutable truth that biology need not define your destiny. You have control over how you want to be and what desires you want to achieve. With a bit of patience, hard work, and commitment, it is possible to build and develop your self-esteem to high levels. Consequently, your ability to succeed in life will also go up a few notches. Here are some examples of strong and powerful men who managed to overcome the overwhelming challenges of low self-esteem:

John Lennon – As a young adult, this British music star

and co-founder of The Beatles believed that part of him was a loser and the other part of him believed himself to be God Almighty. These conflicting emotions are typical of a man with low self-esteem. He failed in nearly all his tests and exams right through his school and college. He worked hard at building his strengths which, in turn, helped him build and develop his self-esteem to become the music superstar that he became.

Thomas Edison – Yes, absolutely! That famous scientist who is one of the few men with the highest number of patents in his name struggled with low self-esteem. He was physically weak and suffered from multiple health issues. He became deaf as a child. You can only begin to imagine the pain and agony he must have gone through before he rose to superstardom in the world of science.

Therefore, if you are a victim of low self-esteem, you need not fret. There are many ways in which you can raise your self-esteem to align it with your true worth.

Loss of Self-Esteem

If self-esteem is not an inherent trait, then it means it is constructed in our minds through our interactions with the outside world. So, what are the factors that deplete our self-esteem? Many of the factors that affect our self-esteem typically begin in our childhood. Here are some of them:

Constantly disapproving parents and teachers – If the elders always found fault with you and focused on what you didn't do well, your self-esteem is bound to be negatively impacted

Uninvolved parents – The feeling of neglect you face if your parents were excessively busy with their lives and did not have the time and energy to nurture you is a primary reason for low self-esteem.

Conflict among parents - If your parents were always bickering and fighting with each other, your confusion about whose side to take is bound to lead to low self-esteem.

Importance of Self-Esteem

Why is self-esteem important for everyone? Mark Twain said, "No man can be comfortable without his own approval." Oscar Wilde said, "To love yourself is the start of a lifelong romance that never loses its appeal." The value and importance of self-esteem cannot be undermined. Here are some excellent reasons why you must begin to work on your self-esteem right away:

- Self-esteem is one of the primary differences between success and failure, both in your personal and professional life
- Self-esteem drives your outlook on life; high self-esteem gives you a positive outlook and low self-esteem results in a negative outlook.
- Self-esteem directly impacts your self-confidence and assertiveness; when you are certain of your worth, your self-confidence and assertiveness will shine through.
- Self-esteem is something that gets reflected in your physical profile; a man with low self-esteem will hold his head high, and a man with low self-esteem will have his

head hanging in shame or guilt or both
- Self-esteem is the starting point to build respect and dignity in your world
- Self-esteem directly impacts your happiness

Signs of Healthy Self-Esteem:
- The ability to say no firmly
- Confidence
- A positive outlook on life
- Ability to identify and accept both strengths and weaknesses
- Ability to articulate needs clearly and strongly
- Ability to accept criticism positively

Signs of Low Self-Esteem:
- Lack of confidence
- A negative outlook on life
- Inability to articulate needs and desires
- Feelings of anxiety, shame, depression, etc.
- Inability to accept criticism in the right spirit
- A strong belief of being useless and worthless
- Fear of failure

Quiz to Discover Your Current Level of Self-Esteem

Answer these questions honestly, which will help you assess your current level of self-esteem. Once you know which areas need to be addressed, you can work on improving them:

Q1. It is very easy for me to feel hurt
1. Most of the time   2. Sometimes   3. Almost never

Q2. Even if I know and believe that someone is giving me constructive criticism, I get hurt and angry.
1. Most of the time   2. Sometimes   3. Almost never

Q3. I get angry with myself even if I make an understandable and acceptable mistake
1. Most of the time   2. Sometimes   3. Almost never

Q4. I ask other people about the decisions I must take instead of making my own decisions
1. Most of the time   2. Sometimes   3. Almost never

Q5. I always accept my team's decision even if I don't agree with them
1. Most of the time   2. Sometimes   3. Almost never

Q6. I am uncomfortable receiving praise and compliments
1. Most of the time   2. Sometimes   3. Almost never

Q7. I don't feel good enough often, and I feel 'I don't really measure up' to my peers.
1. Most of the time   2. Sometimes   3. Almost never

Q8. I engage in negative self-talk, often telling myself things like, "I don't deserve that promotion in the office," or "I can never complete the report on time."

1. Most of the time   2. Sometimes   3. Almost never

Q9. When I see myself in the mirror, I tell myself, "How ugly I am!"
1. Most of the time   2. Sometimes   3. Almost never

Q10. I find myself saying sorry frequently, even if the mistake is not mine.
1. Most of the time   2. Sometimes   3. Almost never

Analyzing your self-discovery quiz - If most of the answers to the above questions are 'almost never,' then your self-esteem level is healthy. Everyone feels uncertain and angry at some point in their life, especially if they don't like what they see. As long as these negative experiences don't happen often, your self-esteem is quite healthy.

If most of your answers were 'sometimes,' then you could be at risk of entering low self-esteem levels, although you may not really be suffering from psychological problems like depression. However, you do tend to have a pessimistic view of yourself, and life in general, which is not a good sign. It might be wise to buckle up and get your self-esteem up. It might even be a good idea to seek professional help.

If most of your answers were 'almost never,' then this is a real cause for concern, and it makes sense to approach a professional and seek help immediately before things reach irreversible levels.

Chapter 2: The Components of Building Self-Esteem

Men need a healthy dose of self-esteem to achieve their best potential in their personal and professional lives. Healthy self-esteem will help you do exceedingly well in your profession, earn well-deserving accolades, and get promotions, and consequently lots more money.

At home too, a healthy dose of self-esteem will make your loved ones feel proud of you. They will love and adore you for who you are without feeling bad about your shortcomings, because you have chosen to accept your weaknesses with humility and an approach to improve yourself.

Nathanial Branden is known as one of the most famous and influential writers about self-esteem and its importance for success and happiness. His most famous book is called *'The Six Pillars of Self-Esteem,'* in which he extols the six components that make up this critical personality trait. The six components of self-esteem include:

1. Conscious living
2. Self-acceptance
3. Self-responsibility
4. Self-assertiveness
5. Living with purpose
6. Personal integrity

Knowing and understanding each of the six components will help you develop your self-esteem wholesomely.

The Practice of Living Consciously

Most of us are drifting along our life paths, simply accepting what comes our way, and then finding reasons for resentment and unhappiness. For example, you get up each morning, brush, wash, dress, have breakfast, and commute to work Are you conscious of the sensations and feelings associated with these routine activities? Do you recall the experience of brushing your teeth or having a bath? Do you recall the taste, texture, and color of the dish you had during breakfast? Do you recall hugging your wife and children with happiness and joy?

Most of us don't even consider these routine activities as important, let alone trying to do them consciously. Living consciously means being in the moment at all times. Living consciously means you are immersed in and engaged with your life knowing and feeling your desires and purposes. Living consciously means focusing all your energies deliberately and purposefully towards achieving your dreams and desires. Here are some great tips to live consciously:

Embrace your true self; warts and all – Don't try to lie to yourself about the kind of person you are. If you are great at managing people, accept this quality with pride, not arrogance. If you have a problem controlling your finances, then accept this quality with humility and without rancor.

Be aware of how you spend your time and energy – Focus on your thoughts and where your attention is going. When you are working on a report at your office, is your entire attention on that task or is your mind wandering to the office party that took place last week even as your hand moves mechanically over the keyboard typing out the important report?

When you are in a project meeting, is your undivided attention in the meeting or has your mind wandered to your child's school report card? When you are doing a task, be conscious of whether that task is contributing to your success, or is it something that is quite irrelevant to it? This focused approach to each element in your life will ensure you don't waste these two precious and depleting resources: time and energy.

Build self-awareness – What are the priorities in your life? Is it your career, your family, health, love of travel and adventure, making money, or anything else? This increased self-awareness will help you understand whether your activities and way of life are aligned with your life purposes or not.

The Practice of Self-Acceptance

Self-acceptance means accepting yourself the way you are

without being judgmental. For example, you are great at people management and everyone in your family and office come to you to solve conflicts. However, you fall short when it comes to computer skills. Simply accept both these qualities without liking or disliking them.

Self-acceptance is a trait that allows you to be who you are without the need for external approval. When you accept yourself, you are merely being okay with who you are at that point in time. It does not mean you are unwilling to change and work on your weaknesses.

Accepting yourself, warts and all, only means you are at a particular point right now, and you are fine with it and have no regrets about being there. However, self-acceptance does not mean you are going to remain there. In fact, self-acceptance is the first step to making positive changes for self-improvement. Here are a few tips to help you achieve self-acceptance:

List your negative aspects and let them go – This approach will help you look at your weaknesses without judgment even as you let go of them. Forgive and show compassion to yourself as you let the judgmental attitudes about your weaknesses go.

Acknowledge your feelings – For example, if your boss said something hurtful to you, then accept the feeling of being hurt. You don't have to react to the feeling. But you should also not suppress the emotion. Don't think about who is wrong or right. Merely accept the pain of the emotion.

Don't be scared of failure – Make failure your ally, because nothing is a better teacher than failure. Failures contribute significantly to our lowered self-esteem. If you accept failure as an opportunity instead of a shaming act, then your self-esteem will not be hit badly.

The Practice of Self-Responsibility

You have learned to live consciously and to accept yourself the way you are. Now, it is time to take responsibility to make positive changes for yourself. Self-responsibility is an attribute given to people who don't view themselves as victims of external circumstances. Instead, they learn to take responsibility and act in a manner that will bring about positive changes in their lives.

For example, if you are poor at computer skills, you cannot blame the computer world for that, can you? Or, for that matter, you cannot play the victim card and say that no one is teaching you. That is a sure sign of low self-esteem. It is up to you to enroll in a computer class or find an online course that you can do at your convenience or find any other resource to build your skills.

The more you learn on your own, the better you get at that skill. People who refuse to help you are actually doing you a favor by increasing your self-reliance. By facing a situation in which you have to learn a skill to survive, you will be driven to learn it in the most effective way possible, ensuring you are on top of the game.

Self-responsibility also includes taking responsibility for your happiness. If you say that the dinner your wife cooked was bad and that made you unhappy, then that is playing the victim card. An alternate solution would be perhaps to order dinner or better still, cook yourself. It is highly likely that your wife will learn from you and improve her cooking skills.

Self-responsibility begins with the awareness that you can take control of your life. There should be no one else but you who is on the driver's seat of your life. It also includes the awareness of the elements in your life that you have no control over.

For example, you are late for work already, and the bus also arrives late. The control to be on time to work is in your hands. However, the control of making the bus come on time is really not in your hands. In such a scenario, you must include the factor of the late-coming of the bus as part of your control by leaving early from home to catch an earlier commute.

As you learn to live consciously, you will become increasingly aware of elements that are under your control and those that are not under your control. Some tips to take on self-responsibility:

- Accept that you are responsible for your thoughts, words, feelings, responses, and everything your body and mind are involved in. Your thoughts are coming from your mind, words from your mouth, feelings from your heart and mind, and so forth. No one can make you do, think, or say something unless you choose to do, think or say.
- Stop blaming and complaining about everyone around you including yourself. Blaming is the ultimate weapon of a victim. It also robs you of the power to change the situation for the better.
- Avoid taking issues personally. The world does not

revolve around you. This attitude will help you take disagreements in your stride without feeling as if you are being personally attacked

The Practice of Self-Assertiveness

The practice of self-assertiveness comes when you live your life by your values and principles, by honoring your needs and desires to achieve your personal goals and life purposes. So, you start your journey of building self-esteem by first learning to live consciously, then accepting yourself as who you are, followed by taking responsibility for what is happening in your life and your happiness. The next component of self-esteem is to identify, honor, and assert your needs and desires.
Self-assertiveness is also referred to as authenticity which means you are projecting your true inner self to the outside world. Additionally, self-assertiveness includes your ability to articulate your needs and desires to the world when the need arises.

For example, if honesty is a crucial value in your life, then speaking, behaving, and standing for honesty should be your primary focus even in the face of rising unpopularity for your actions. Fear of aversion should not drive you away from your life's values and principles.

Therefore, living with self-assertiveness is, perhaps, one of the most difficult self-esteem components to achieve. Living consciously will make you realize that it is far easier to give in to popular demands (against your values and principles) than to be self-assertive.

For example, a big promotion is coming up and you don't want to displease your boss. He repeatedly calls you into work on weekends. You have promised to take your kids on a family picnic one weekend after letting your boss know that you will not come into work. He agrees, but again on Friday he demands that you come to work the next day.

Do you stand by your promise to your kids or do you break the promise to please your boss and increase your chances of getting that coveted promotion? These dilemmas will keep raising their ugly heads in your life and challenging your self-assertiveness. Your ability to withstand the challenges and come out unscathed is what will define your level of self-esteem.

The Practice of Living with Purpose

When you have a purpose in life, you don't merely exist. A definitive reason behind the 'why' of your life drives you to use your passion and talents to thrive in a happy and meaningful life. Winston Churchill said, *"It is not enough to have simply lived. We should be determined to live for something."*

A purpose in your life gives you determination and focus to stay on your goal path. This forward march towards a set goal is a huge contributor to self-esteem. As you progress on your journey and measure the progress and see how close you are getting to your goal, you will raise your self-esteem a few notches.

If you are a man who is struggling to find purpose in life, don't fret. You are one amongst millions of other men going through a similar situation. That you have woken up to the fact that you lack a purpose is the first step to finding your purpose. The earlier you work on your life purpose, the easier it will be for you to get a direction in life.

Each of us has different purposes and you should not be compelled to follow anyone else's path except your own. There are no right and wrong purposes in life too. *"People take different paths for happiness and fulfillment. Just because they are not on your path does not mean they have got lost,"* says the Dalai Lama.

Therefore, it is imperative that you find your purpose for yourself. While you can take the advice and suggestions of well-wishers, the ultimate decision should be yours and yours alone. Take self-responsibility for your life purpose. Here are some tips to find your life purpose:

Identify your strengths – Make a list of things you are reasonably good at and a list of things in which you are exceptional. In fact, you could be so good at some things that you wonder why others find it difficult to do. It could be anything including an amazing ability to read people, to merely glance at balance sheets and find mistakes, a skill at being extremely detailed, a great communicator, or anything else.

Identify your passion – What do you care deeply about? Nelson Mandela said, *"There is no passion in living* *small; in choosing a life that is less than what you are capable of."* You don't have to have a fire in your belly to find your passion or live a meaningful life of purpose. You don't have to be driven by a deep desire to start an orphanage or old-age home. Of course, if you have this desire, go right ahead and do it.

However, on a practical level, identify what triggers your emotions, what lights you up, and what gives you a sense of peace. If you still have problems with finding your passion, simply start by writing down who and what you care about. What is closest to your heart? And move forward from there.

Find out where and in what you add the most value – Identifying what you serve best is the final step to finding your purpose. Ask yourself these questions:
• What kind of problems are you great at solving?
• What kinds of needs of other people can you easily meet?
• Who are the people you are best placed to serve?
• What kind of struggles can you help ease in other people?
• Where is the place you continuously add value?

The ideas that are at the junction of the above three points will give you a direction to your life purpose.

The Practice of Personal Integrity

Now that five of the six components of self-esteem are covered, you are well on your way to building healthy lf-esteem. The final and, perhaps, the largest to self-esteem is personal integrity. Personal lects your ability to lead a life that is aligned with your values and principles. Living by your values enhances your self-belief that you are sufficiently equipped to lead your life on your terms and using your skills and strengths.

Take that example of having to stand up to your boss and asserting yourself so that you can keep your promise of taking your children for a weekend picnic. Now, your personal integrity will come into play here. For example, if your life purpose is your career and you are driven by your personal integrity, then you choose to become unpopular with your children and give in to the demands of your boss. Alternately, if your life purpose and value is driven by family and loved ones, then by showcasing your personal integrity, you choose to incur the wrath of your boss by standing your ground and saying you will not come into the office that particular weekend and, perhaps, lower your chances of promotion.

So, there are no right and wrong answers to life's questions. Your actions and behaviors will make some people happy and some people unhappy. The crucial element for personal integrity is to ask yourself if you are reflecting your true self to the outside world or are you pretending to do something simply to please people. The former behavior rates your personal integrity at a high level.

When you choose to reject your personal values and stray from the path of personal integrity, it is quite likely that, for a little while, the people you tried to please are happy with your choice. However, sooner rather than later, you will find this conflicting behavior affecting your life negatively, because not living your life on your terms is equal to rejecting yourself, which is the first step to lowered self-esteem.

So, working on the six components as propounded by Nathaniel Branden gives you the perfect direction to build and develop your self-esteem. Take the following quizzes on the six components to understand your current levels.

Self-Assessment Questionnaire for Living Consciously

The following questions are based on Neuro-Linguistic Programming techniques that help you understand your current level of living consciously. Each of the questions (from Q1-Q6) should be answered with one of the following options:

A. I don't sense anything, and I am not aware

B. Sometimes I do sense, but I don't know how to control them

C. I can sense clearly and vividly

Q1. Do you see visuals in your mind?

Q2. Do you hear your inner voices clearly?

Q3. Do you connect with your feelings and emotions deeply?

Q4. Do you recognize and identify people, situations, and your own inner thoughts that trigger your reactions?

Q5. Do you know your limitations?

Q6. Do you sense your inner conflicts?

For the next set of 4 questions, write down your answers in

detail:

Q7. Have you identified your personal beliefs and values? What are they?

Q8. What is the thing you value the most in your life and why?

Q9. How do the people in your life, including family and loved ones, friends, social circle, and co-workers impact your life?

Q10. What are your strengths and weaknesses?

Self-Assessment Questionnaire for Self-Acceptance

Q1. Are your life goals based on your needs and desires?

Q2. Are you always comparing your capabilities with those of others?

Q3. Are you always trying to grade your work and yourself as good, bad, average, not enough?

Q4. If your work is criticized, do you feel bad about it?

Q5. Are you always thinking about your weaknesses and rarely giving yourself credit for your strengths?

Self-Assessment Questionnaire for Self-Responsibility

Q1. Do you think that your behaviors, reactions, and responses are your own?

Q2. Do you accept responsibility for your behaviors and reactions, even if you know that something outside of you caused them?

Q3. Do you accept responsibility for your physical and mental health?

Q4. Do you accept that only you are responsible for your happiness?

Q5. Do you believe that your values and principles should

be your own and not borrowed from other people who influence your life?

Self-Assessment Questionnaire for Self-Assertiveness

Q1. Do you make an effort to do what you believe in, even if means being unpopular with the people who love and care for you?

Q2. Do you live your life the way you want to?

Q3. Suppose you are forced to go a party because of some obligation, do you think how you spend the time there is entirely in your control?

Q4. Do you ask for help when you know you need it?

Self-Assessment Questionnaire for Purposeful Living

Q1. Where do you see your career five years from now? Do you see growth? What kind of growth?

Q2. Do you have different sets of goals for different aspects of your life? Are they all time-bound, measurable, and achievable?

Q3. How do you keep track of progress for your different goals?

Q4. What are the elements that hinder your progress and what are those that facilitate your progress towards your goals?

Self-Assessment Questionnaire for Personal Integrity

Q1. How often do you lie to people, both in your personal and professional life? Why do you choose to lie?

Q2. Suppose you realize you have made a mistake at your office. You have an easy way to get away without being caught. However, someone else ends up taking the blame. What will you do?

Q3. Are you leading a life that is perfectly aligned with your values and principles? If it is perfect, what and where are the deviations?

Chapter 3: Habits and How to Use Them for Good

Human beings are creatures of habits, and we don't know how to live without them. Reflect on a typical day at home, and you will see that nearly 90% of what you do is habitual in nature. We are unwittingly replacing old habits with new ones regularly. Habits can typically be divided into:
1. Indiscernible habits, such as tying shoelaces, bathing, brushing your teeth, etc.
2. Bad habits, such as overeating, smoking, putting off work, addictions, etc.
3. Good habits, such as daily exercise, eating nutritiously, getting a good night's rest each day, etc.

Everyone wants to build good habits and eliminate bad habits in their life. One way of doing this is to look at each bad habit, find its trigger, and work at it individually to break it or convert it into a good habit. For example, you can look at the bad habit of smoking and understand how it works in your body and mind, and break it slowly and steadily, or replace it with, perhaps, chewing gum, which is less harmful than smoking. Each habit needs to be handled differently and calls for different techniques to break (the bad ones) and build (the good ones).

In an attempt to bring all kinds of habits under one umbrella, Charles Duhigg, supported by years of research and surveys, came out with a book called, *'The Power of Habit,'* in which he discusses the habit loop in detail. You can take any habit of yours and fit it into this habit loop. Understanding the habit loop will enlighten you on how habit work. Once you comprehend this concept, then you can attack any bad habit and convert it into a good one, or simply eliminate it from your life.

The habit loop, as per Charles Duhigg, consists of:
- The Cue
- The Routine
- The Reward

The Cue

Also referred to as the trigger, this element puts your brain into the habit mode and compels it to perform the habit action (or the Routine). Cues can be of different types. Let us look at some of them:

Time cue – This is the most common form of cues for setting the habit routine in motion. For example, at around noon, you automatically reach out for your lunch. At around 3pm, you habitually step out for a coffee. Let us use this cue to understand the trigger of a bad habit.

Suppose you are to step out after lunch to meet your buddies at the cigarette shop for a smoke. This is at around 12.15 after lunch. From today, be conscious of your feelings at 12.15 after your lunch. What are your feelings? The urge for a cigarette? The desire to be with your friends?

Boredom or loneliness because there is nothing to do or nobody to talk to after having your lunch until your break time is over?

Study this cue in detail. Suppose it was an urge for a cigarette. Understand your emotions layer by layer. Is there a physical pain if you don't have your cigarette? If yes, then it is possible that you need professional help to get out of this habit. However, if there is no physical pain, then analyze your urge for the cigarette. Can it be replaced with chewing gum? Or a cup of coffee? Or something else harmful? Can you move your lunchtime to 1pm instead of 12 noon? Will that make a difference to break the habit.

If the time cue drives the urge to be with friends, then can you find another place to meet them instead of the cigarette shop? If you are bored or lonely, can you identify someone in your office with whom you can share your lunch? Or can you carry a novel or book you can read during that time?

The primary lesson is that, by studying the time cue, you are consciously trying to understand how and what is driving you to the bad habit. When you know that element, you can find ways to break it or replace it with something that can start off a good habit instead of a bad one.

Location cue – Many times, being at a particular place sets off the bad habit. In the smoking example, the cigarette shop could be the trigger to buy yourself a cigarette and start smoking. So, to change that, change the location of the post-lunch meeting with your friends. Try a juice bar or a café which does not sell cigarettes. Alternately, carry a small pack of chewing gum (make sure it is the sugar-free ones) with you, and pick one from the pack instead of buying a cigarette.

Preceding events cue – What happens when your phone rings? You answer the call, and when it is over, you automatically scan through your notifications, right? That is a classic example of a preceding event cue. When you get the call, your brain is habituated into checking for notifications.

Now, on a busy day at your office, this habit can eat into a lot of time reducing your productivity and efficiency considerably. You must be conscious of it and battle it out with your brain not to scan notifications after answering the call. Alternately, keep notifications off while you are working. Then, there will be nothing to see.

You can use the preceding event cue to set up good habits. For example, your morning coffee is almost a done thing. Now, set up a habit of meditating for a couple of minutes after you finish your coffee. Another example would be before retiring to bed, use the sleeping time as a cue to make entries in your daily journal or create your to-do list for the next day.

Emotional status cue – Have you gone out drinking whenever something bad happened at your workplace? Do you reach for the bottle in the evening when your boss has criticized you? Your emotional status is one of the most common cues to trigger bad habits.

Emotions are always more difficult to overcome than time, location, and preceding events cues. Emotions can become so powerful that they tend to overwhelm us and the ability to act rationally reduces considerably. One of the most effective methods to manage emotions is to engage in some form of mood-enhancing activity, such as hitting the gym or going for a run. Use a punching bag to transfer your anger and sadness.

Another way to cope with overwhelming emotions is to practice mindfulness. By being mindfully aware of your emotions, you are allowing your body to feel the rush of anger or sadness and helping yourself from reacting in a regrettable way. Learn some basic and simple breathing exercises that facilitate a mindful state.

The company you keep – For example, if you spend every Friday evening with people who enjoy drinking, you are also going to be drinking. Avoid going out with this set of friends, at least on Friday evening when you know a booze session is bound to start with them.

Similarly, if you are having lunch with someone who eats excessively, you will also be driven to overeat. So, if you are trying to break the habit of overeating, avoid friends who tend to eat more than you should. Stick with people who consume sparse meals.

Surround yourself with people who keep good habits if you want to build good habits. And stay away from people who indulge in bad habits, and your resolve to get rid of them will become stronger than before.

The Routine

The routine in a habit loop is the actual action performed.

For example, when you take that post-lunch break with your friends to smoke, the act of smoking itself is the routine. Looking up social media notifications after you complete your phone call is an example of the routine. Here are some ways you can alter the routines so that bad habits can become good habits:
- Replace the cigarette with fruit
- Replace the cigarette with your favorite book
- Use preceding events to remind you of good habit routines
- Meditate during emotional stress

The Reward

The reward is the final prize or the end-result of the habit loop. The brain decides the value of the habit based on the quality of the reward. For example, the joy of drinking is the reward for habitual drinkers. The brains of drinkers are habituated into storing, keeping track of, and recalling cues that trigger drinking because the joy of drinking is worthy of the effort.

Other rewards discussed in this chapter include:
- The thrill of reading useless but exciting gossip on social media
- The joy of overeating
- The joy of spending time with friends
- The calming (though temporary) effect of the alcohol

Changing bad habits to good ones can happen if you experiment with rewards. For example, you can try to meditate for a couple of minutes every time you complete a phone call. The stress-busting joy of even these short-duration meditations can give you the same but more productive joy of reading useless but exciting gossip on social media.

Make sure you have fruit handy wherever you so that you can overeat them to your heart's content, doing far less harm than overeating pizzas and burgers. The joy of spending time with friends can hardly be replaced. However, you can get the same joy if you can change the venue of your meeting place. How about meeting at the local gym and spending quality time with friends, even as you burn some calories in the process.

The calming effect of alcohol can easily be replaced by more sustainable rewards such as the peace of meditation, the stress-busting techniques associated with mindfulness living, or simply charging up your pheromones by hitting the gym or going for a run in the neighborhood park.

Therefore, follow the habit loop for all your habits, and make suitable changes at any or all of the three places (cue, routine, or reward) and replace your bad habits with good ones and enhance the quality of your life. With improved quality of life comes improved self-esteem driven by the results of doing things the right way.

Self-Discovery of Bad Habits

Here is a small (definitely not exhaustive) list of bad habits that men frequently get trapped by. Look at each of them and see if you are already in the throes or carry the risk of becoming addicted to that bad habit.

- Excessive eating and/or drinking
- Procrastinating
- Being late for an appointment or meeting
- Picking your nose or teeth in public
- Overuse of bad words
- Checking your mobile device in the middle of dinner
- Eating sloppily or with your mouth open
- Never picking up the tab when eating out with friends
- Snapping or popping gum in public
- Talking (even whispering) during a movie
- Not helping in the kitchen
- Addiction to social media, video games, YouTube videos
- Binge-watching TV serials or movies

Avoid putting off catching these and other bad habits and throwing them out of your life. The longer you put off this critical activity, the more difficult it will become because the habit is getting increasingly ingrained into your psyche with each passing day.

Step-by-Step Guide to Eliminate Bad Habits or Replace them with Good Ones

Step 1 - Identify one bad habit you intend to break. Start with the easiest one because the success from this will motivate you to try a harder next time. What are the cues for it? Who are the people around you at that time? What time does this cue typically get triggered? What are your emotions at that time?

Step 2 – What is the reward or craving that you find irresistible? Try other rewards that can result in the same satisfaction without the associated habit-forming negative side-effects. Experimenting with rewards should be an ongoing process. Keep trying until you have quit the bad habit.

Step 3 – Now, define the new routine with the new rewards. Put the new habit loop in place. Additionally, you must put up reminders and sticky-notes in obvious places until your brain becomes accustomed to the new habit.

Here is an example of setting a new habit: Before going to bed (the preceding event cue), I will make the to-do list (routine) for the next day. The result of being prepared and organized is the reward.

Here is an example of replacing old bad habits with new good ones: For my post-lunch (time cue) meet with my friends (the routine and reward), I will change the venue from the cigarette shop (old location) to the nearby park (new location) for a short game of baseball.

Alain De Botton, the renowned British philosopher, coach, and counselor, says, *"The best cure for your bad habits is to see it in action in another person."* Don't ever underestimate the debilitating harm an unresolved bad habit can cause. Work at it and root it out of your system.

Chapter 4: Practical Examples

This chapter gives you some practical examples of how you can work on the six components discussed in Chapter 2 to build and develop your self-esteem.

The Practice of Living Consciously

NLP Techniques
Neuro-Linguistic Programming (NLP) is a technique that is designed to align your conscious mind with your subconscious and unconscious mind. NLP techniques are proven to help in improving mindset, memory, intelligence, and communication skills. Here are some NLP techniques to help you lead a more conscious life:

Pay close attention to your thoughts – Our subconscious and unconscious minds are affected deeply by our thoughts. For example, if you have a presentation on Monday morning, and your thoughts are, "I know I'm going to a bad job," or "I think I am going to goof up big time on Monday," then your subconscious mind will send subtle signs to your body and conscious mind to resist your efforts to prepare well for the presentation.

On the contrary, if your thoughts are, "I'm sure I will be a hit with my presentation. I know I have taken care of all the details needed to make it a perfect piece," then your subconscious mind will tell your gross mind and body to work hard and ensure the presentation comes out perfectly on the D-day.

Don't forget to pray – Prayers to a supernatural being whom you believe is more endowed and more capable than you are nothing but hopes and self-wishes for good things to happen. Prayers render a strong sense of faith which drives you to work hard to achieve your wish.

For example, if you want that bonus really hard this year, then you pray every day to get it. Your conscious mind accepts the prayers and passes it on to the subconscious mind which will drive you to accept the importance and criticality of this prayer. The faith that spreads through your entire being will drive you to work hard to realize your dreams.

Affirmations – Affirmations are like mantras. The more you repeat, the deeper it gets ingrained into your psyche, which creates a positive aura around you leaving you powerful and strong to get what you want. Some examples of every day positive affirmations for living consciously:
- I accept responsibility for my life
- I am a wise, intelligent, and conscious human being
- I live a disciplined and balanced life
- I don't need other people's approval to be happy
- I do all my tasks with my heart, body, and soul
- I accept what I can control and also what I cannot

control
- I have limitless potential and I can expand and grow to the best of my abilities

Visualization techniques – Visualization and imagination help you stay on the path of your goal without being negatively affected by external factors. There are multiple benefits of visualization, or the happy moment or joy of achieving your dream. One of the primary benefits of visualization is that it helps you reach your maximum potential.

For example, if you can visualize running a 10K marathon, you might not suddenly become physically powerful to run a record time the next day. However, your subconscious mind will be driven to accept the reality of your imagination, and in turn, compel you to reach your maximum potential.

So, if you have an important presentation to give, visualize the success of your efforts and everyone lauding your work. It will help strengthen your resolve and motivation to really do well.

Meditation – Meditation is one of the most effective tools for living consciously. Meditation helps you connect with your deepest thoughts and emotions. In such a circumstance, you will be able to discern between the various emotions and understand the true nature of your thoughts.

Meditation helps you to remain in the moment so that your heart, mind, and soul are all synchronized together to give you a fabulously resonating experience in every single moment of your life.

Maintaining a diary – Making entries in your diary every day enhances your ability to live more consciously than before. Write down three positive and negative experiences of each day. Include the following details for each event:

- Details of the event
- Who were the other people present?
- When did it happen?
- What were your feelings?
- What were the lessons learned?

Many times, we get so emotionally caught up in a life experience that we cannot truly differentiate between the various emotions at that point. However, later on, when you are trying to record the event when it is fresh in the mind, you will find it easier to discern the different emotions that you felt.

For example, if your presentation went well, you would have felt a general sense of happiness. But, when you make an effort to write down the feelings, you will be able to recall other emotions and thoughts such as pride, relief, increased self-confidence, the resolve to take on more challenges in the future, and more. Additionally, you will be able to treat your negative experiences objectively, allowing you to take as many lessons as you can from them.

Therefore, maintaining a diary with daily entries will help you relive your experiences more consciously than before.

The Practice of Self-Acceptance

NLP Techniques

Anchoring technique – This NLP technique helps you anchor your positive experiences using physical sensations. Recall one of the most favorite and happiest moments of your life. Now, as you recall those positive emotions, touch the tip of your forefinger to the tip of your thumb. By doing this, you are anchoring that happy experience to this particular gesture.

Whenever you are going through a phase of self-doubt, touch the tip of your forefinger to the tip of your thumb, and recall that joyful time again, and watch your self-doubt disappear. With repeated practice of this anchoring technique, you will notice that every time you bring the tips of your forefinger and thumb together, automatically your thoughts will go to that joyful experience. It's a perfect technique to shake off any feelings of self-doubt and biased criticism quickly.

Affirmations – Use the following affirmations for self-acceptance. Repeat them as often as you can, and definitely when you wake up in the morning to start off your day on a positive note.

- I deserve happiness, joy, and love
- I unconditionally accept and love myself the way I am
- I am complete on my own and do not need any external factors to make me feel whole.
- I will use this gift of life exuberantly and confidently

Visualization Techniques

Imagine yourself as happy and joyful at all times. Imagine you are always smiling irrespective of external circumstances. When you visualize a happy scene, your subconscious mind will accept it to be the truth and compel your gross body and conscious mind to work towards converting that visual image into reality.

When you love and accept yourself visually, it will be reflected in your body language as well. There will be a spring in your step, a smile on your face, and a positive aura around you. People naturally gravitate towards happy people. Therefore, your positivity will attract more people to you helping you build your level of self-confidence and self-esteem.

Meditation

Use the self-acceptance affirmations given above to meditate and increase the feel-good emotion in your life. When you are going through an emotionally tumultuous time, and you are unsure of yourself, find a quiet place where you will not be disturbed for about 5-10 minutes, close your eyes, and focus on your breath even as you repeat a suitable affirmation.

For example, if you are nervous before a presentation, and a nasty colleague passes a rude comment hoping to stifle your confidence, don't give in to the negative emotions flooding your body. Smile at your colleague, go out of the office, find a peaceful place to meditate and repeat the affirmation, "I am a confident person, and I approve of myself. I do not get discouraged by external factors." When the emotions have drained from your system, you will find yourself feeling noticeably more confident and not feeling bitter against your colleague. Self-acceptance makes you increasingly compassionate towards others.

Maintaining a Diary

Write down the talents and skills that you are proud of and the weaknesses you want to work on. Answer the following questions about yourself which will help you increase self-acceptance:

- Do I want the best for myself? Will I ever cheat myself? What should I do to trust myself more?
- What are the good things happening in my life that I know for certain I deserve? Why do I believe I deserve these good things?
- Suppose you did not get that promotion you were hoping to get last month. Were you disappointed? Why? Now, after a month, can you think of at least one good reason why you believe not getting that promotion was actually a good thing?

The Practice of Self-Responsibility

NLP Techniques
The NLP Swish technique – The Swish technique helps you replace a negative thought with a positive one so that your brain uses the same trigger to think positively. The Swish technique has the following elements:

- Unwanted thoughts and triggers
- Unwanted feelings
- Replacement thought

Let us take an example in your professional life where you

can successfully use this NLP technique. Suppose you appeared for a promotion interview last year, and you were not selected for promotion. The same opportunity has come up again, and you want to go for the interview again. You have performed exceedingly well the last year, and your boss is pleased with you. You have brushed up your technical knowledge too and have updated yourself with the latest skills required for the new role you are applying for.

Yet, you are filled with apprehension driven by last year's failure. So, how can you replace the negativity with positivity using the Swish technique? Here's is what you should do:

Unwanted thoughts – are those that trigger a negative feeling in you. The thoughts could be visions of you failing again this year.

Unwanted feelings – are those emotions of fear and uncertainty

Replacement thoughts – You have undergone multiple mock interviews with your boss and your peers. You have done exceedingly well in many of them. Take an example of one such successful mock interview (preferably done with your boss) in which he or she has praised you for your efforts and said positive things about the potential outcome of the real interview.

Replace the unwanted thoughts with this positive and happy memory and relive that experience until the unwanted feelings are eliminated from your heart and mind. Use the NLP Swish technique to get rid of baseless self-doubts and fears and be prepared to face challenges with confidence.

Affirmations

Take responsibility for building and developing self-esteem, because no one else can really do it for you. Use any of the following affirmations to increase self-acceptance:

- I am totally responsible for my self-esteem and I will give my 100% to build it
- I am responsible for whatever is happening in my life
- I take responsibility for all my actions, behaviors, words, and everything I do or say
- I am not responsible for how others behave with me

Visualization Techniques

Visualization is a very strong tool to build your future in your mind which is then transmitted by the subconscious mind to your entire being driving you to give your best to make that visualization a reality. Here is an example of visualization for self-acceptance:

- Sit comfortably in a quiet, undisturbed place.
- Close your eyes and imagine yourself entering your office elevator with confidence
- Visualize a happy smile on your face and well-groomed profile.
- Imagine getting into the elevator and being greeted by colleagues and subordinates
- Visualize yourself responding with equal gusto
- Next, visualize yourself getting off from the elevator and crossing the long corridor to your cabin, nodding and greeting people on the way
- Next, visualize passing your boss' cabin, and

peeping in to wish him or her good morning and receiving a positive greeting in return.

• Imagine a spring in your step as you get into your cabin and switch on the computer to get started for the day A positive visualization such as this will help you get off to a great start.

Meditation

Look at this illustration. You have joined a local gym, and you have taken on the services of a dedicated trainer to help you with your fitness. Now, one day, you are lifting weights, and your trainer tells you to start with something heavier than the previous time. You are a bit hesitant, but your trainer tells you that if you are cautious, then it will be alright. So, you go ahead and listen to him.

Unfortunately, you pull a muscle while lifting the heavier weights as recommended by your trainer. You could, of course, blame your trainer for suggesting the idea. However, instead of reacting rashly, sit and meditate and focus your thoughts on the entire episode, and the following glaring ideas will come to the fore:

• Your lack of conviction in letting your trainer know that you are not ready for heavier weights

• Your loss of concentration when you pulled the muscles

• Acting with undue bravado

• Ignoring the pain that the initial couple of lifts gave you thinking it was normal

Meditating and focusing on the episode opened new vistas, giving you the required leeway to handle yourself in a calm, cool, and mature manner. This kind of attitude enhances your popularity, resulting in increased self-esteem.

Maintaining a Diary
Every day, make a note of two experiences that you did not like. Next to each one of them, write down at least two things you could have done to reduce the negative impact of the experience. As you practice of this exercise, you will find it increasingly easy to take onus for all that is happening to you.

The Practice of Self-Assertiveness

NLP Techniques
One of the primary and most effective ways of asserting yourself is learning to say no. Look back at your professional life and list the number of times you should have ideally said no to your co-worker or boss or subordinate. Instead, you said yes, and have been trapped in your own cage, unable to wriggle out of problems.

Next time that bossy subordinate asks for leave, firmly say no to her. Get it right once, and you will be surprised how easy it is to a much more productive and efficient level of work than before. NLP techniques include deconstructing and formulating various scenarios in which you will practice mentally to say no, so that when the real thing happens, your mind is ready for the challenge.

Affirmations
Some self-assertive affirmations for you:
- I am fearless and speak my mind
- I am a self-assertive man
- I can easily articulate my opinions and feelings to

people
- I am a confident person
- I stand firm when the situation calls for it.

Visualization Techniques
Let us take the example of having to say no to your bossy subordinate next time she asks for leave with a valid reason. Here are some steps to help you visualize the scene:
- Imagine the lady walking into your cabin and asking for leave
- Visualize yourself making eye contact with her and looking confidently at her
- Imagine her discomfiture at this new attitude of yours
- Visualize yourself asking her for a valid reason for her leave request
- Imagine her struggling to come up with something
- Visualize yourself giving her an alternative that she simply cannot refuse
- Visualize her leaving your cabin humbly accepting defeat

Repeat this visualization in your mind until the fears of standing up and saying no disappear completely.

Meditation
Meditation is the perfect solution for self-assertiveness because it empowers you to see various perspectives of the same situation using which you can come up with multiple options to overcome nearly all challenges in your life effectively. Meditation teaches you to differentiate between assertiveness and aggression, thereby giving you the power

to assert yourself without hurting other people.

Meditation enhances your self-awareness which, in turn, helps you articulate your needs unhesitatingly. Make meditation a daily habit. Spend about 15 minutes with yourself, learning to be comfortable in your own company. There are many occasions that you can find during the day to meditate. You could use your daily commute time to meditate, you could use your post-lunch walk, you could spend 15 minutes before retiring to bed, or any other convenient time.

Maintaining a Diary

In your diary, make a note of all the challenges you faced that day. Next to each challenge, write down affirmation statements to build your self-assertiveness and prepare yourself, should the occasion arise again. For example, your wife and you had a bitter battle after you returned from work in which she, perhaps, accused you of some untrue things, leaving you humiliated and insulted in front of your children. Without getting into her side of the story, use the following diary entry to recover from that difficult situation:

First, write down all the emotions you felt during the tiff: anger, sadness, resentment, and whatever else. Then, write down the following affirmation a couple of times next to this entry: Lies said in the rudest way or in the loudest voice do not become true. People who lie are only undermining themselves.

The Practice of Living Purposefully

NLP Techniques
Set SMART goals (a powerful and highly beneficial NLP tool) to live your life with purpose. Your goals should be:

S – Specific and not general: for example, 'I will complete the write-up of five of the ten cases allocated to me by the end of this week,' is a valid specific goal for a young lawyer. However, 'I will try to complete as many cases as I can by the end of this week' is not specific.

M – Measurable: for example, in the above case, each time one case write-up is done, the young lawyer can knock it off from his list and measure how many more he has left to complete the goal of 5 per week.

A – Achievable: for example, the young lawyer wanting to become a Supreme Court judge within weeks of getting his law certificate is not achievable

R – Realistic: for example, if the young lawyer had been allocated 50 cases, setting a goal of completing all the 50 within a week seems unrealistic.

T – Timebound: Goals must have a date beyond which they expire if you have failed to achieve them; for example, if the young lawyer had not put '5 cases by the end of this week,' it would is not timebound.

Affirmations
Affirmations for living purposefully:
- I am connected with my life purpose
- I know exactly what I want to achieve
- My inner voice keeps directing me to stay on my

chosen path
- I live a passionate and purposeful life
- I dream big and work very hard to realize those big dreams

Visualization Techniques

Use the following visualization scenes to inch closer to your set goals:
- Visualize getting a promotion and being congratulated by your super-boss
- Visualize getting your boss' cabin allocated to you on promotion
- Visualize a nice increase in your pay
- Visualize a beautiful home by the beach in which you are living happily with your wife and kids
- Visualize going off on an exotic holiday with your family
- Visualize a lovely Thanksgiving dinner at home, surrounded by your loved ones who are looking at you with love and respect

Meditation

Living with a purpose has multiple challenges, and one of the biggest ones is to lose track of your purpose. Meditation is a great way to repeatedly remind yourself of your life goals. Spend a few minutes each day focusing on your purpose and your daily goals.

Maintaining a Diary

It is best to record your SMART goals divided into daily, weekly, and monthly targets into your diary. Record your progressions and hindrances along with solutions that worked for the challenges. You will never lose sight of your ultimate life goal.

The Practice of Personal Integrity

NLP Techniques
Personal integrity is all about showing your true character to the outside world. Here are some NLP-approved techniques to help you practice personal integrity:
- Learn to say NO because it will help you make only those promises that you are certain of delivering
- Learn self-discipline and focus so that you work efficiently and productively doing things that are aligned with your values and not wasting resources that are not aligned with your principles

Affirmations
Some affirmations for personal integrity:
- I promise to be honest and straightforward always
- I will promise only what I can deliver
- I take pride in owning up to my mistakes
- I will stand by my principles even if it means becoming unpopular

Visualization Techniques
Here are some visualization techniques to help build personal integrity:
- Imagine the happy faces of your loved ones when you keep your promises made to them
- Imagine the sad faces of your children when you say that the weekend picnic is going to be canceled because

you need to work over the weekend
- Visualize the joy of your team members when you kept the promise of fighting to get them all a good raise for a job well done

Meditation

Meditation is the best way to get to know ourselves at the deepest level. This increased self-awareness helps us stay committed to our values and principles. Meditate regularly and understand yourself better.

Maintaining a Diary

In your diary, keep a list of broken promises to remind yourself of the pain you caused to the person concerned. When a similar situation arises in which you run the risk of breaking another promise, retrieve your diary and use the entry made in it, especially about the pain in the face of the concerned individual. This will help you work hard and stand by your promise.

Chapter 5: Workbook

The workbook is based on the six components of self-esteem propounded by Nathaniel Branden in his book, 'The Six Pillars of Self-Esteem.' Complete the quizzes and questionnaires given at the end of the various chapters, specifically in Chapter 4. The answers to these questions and quizzes will give you your current status regarding the six components of self-esteem including:

- The practice of living consciously
- The practice of self-acceptance
- The practice of self-responsibility
- The practice of self-assertiveness
- The practice of living purposefully
- The practice of personal integrity

Based on your answers, rank the order of your current status of the six components started from your strongest point and move towards your weakest point. For example, suppose you got the best scores for living consciously and the worst scores for living purposefully. Do this workbook in reverse order. Basically, stand with that component which needs your immediate attention because you are lagging behind on it. Let us dive straight into the workbook

now:
Workbook for the Practice of Living Consciously
NLP techniques – Pay Close Attention to Your Thoughts

Before going to bed, make a note of the three most enervating thoughts that was in your mind constantly today

1)
_____
_____
_____
_____
_____
_____
_____

2)
_____
_____
_____
_____
_____
_____
_____

3)
_____
_____
_____
_____
_____
_____
_____

NLP techniques – Prayers

Every Sunday morning (best time is after you return from church; however, if you don't have a practice of going to church, then before you sit down for your breakfast), make a note of the three most crucial prayers that you definitely want answered during the week:

1)
_____
_____
_____
_____
_____
_____
_____

2)
_____
_____
_____
_____
_____
_____
_____

3)
_____
_____
_____
_____
_____
_____
_____

Affirmations – From the examples given in Chapter 4,

or after researching on your own, make a note of the three affirmations that are best aligned with your choice to live consciously:

1) _____
_____
_____

2) _____
_____
_____

3) _____
_____
_____

Visualization – Visualize the most important purpose in your life and make detailed notes of the imagined scene. Remember to include:

The scene
_____
_____

The people in it
_____

Smells
_____
_____

Sounds
_____
_____

Your feelings
_____

Meditation – Many times, despite our best efforts, some thoughts continue to haunt us right through the meditation session. After your meditation session, make a note of two of the topmost thoughts that refused to leave your mind:

1)
_____
_____
_____
_____
_____
_____

2)
_____
_____
_____
_____
_____
_____

Maintaining a diary – At the end of every week, read your journal entries. Identify at least one item that repeated twice (at a minimum) for which you had to be grateful. Don't stop at one if there are more. Write down all such items:

1)
_____
_____
_____

Workbook for the Practice of Self-Acceptance

NLP anchoring technique - Take two of the most beautiful memories of your life. Use the NLP anchoring technique to create happiness anchors so that you are prepared to use them during an emergency:

1)

2)

Affirmations – Create three affirmations for self-acceptance on your own without referring to the examples given in this book.

1)

2) _____

3) _____

Visualization –Write detailed notes of a situation when you were at your happiest. What happened? And what were the emotions? Who was responsible for giving you this level of happiness?

_____
_____
_____
_____
_____
_____

Meditation – Meditate on any of the following affirmations that you created for yourself for the self-acceptance component:
1) _____
_____

2) _____
_____

Workbook for the Practice of Self-Responsibility

The NLP Swish technique – Make a note of three unwanted thoughts that trigger unwanted feelings. Next to each of these unwanted thoughts, write a replacement thought:

Unwanted	trigger	1)

Replacement	trigger	1)

Unwanted	trigger	2)

Replacement	trigger	2)

Unwanted	trigger	3)

Replacement	trigger	3)

—

Affirmation – Create two your own self-responsibility affirmations?

1) _____
   _____

   _____

2) _____
   _____

   _____

Visualization – What is the most important goal in your life? Visualize the day you will reach this goal. Make detailed notes of your visualization including scenes, smells, the joy of your loved ones, your own emotions, and everything else.

_____
_____
_____
_____
_____
_____
_____

Meditation – Recall a painful experience in your life. Relive the experience and think about it without the associated emotions that were there in the original. Now, make a list of all factors that contributed to the pain. Categorize the factors under two separate headings:
Under your control

_____
_____
_____
_____
_____
_____
_____

Not under your control

_____
_____
_____
_____

_____

_____

You can use your journal entries to identify such painful experiences.

Workbook for the Practice of Self-Assertiveness

NLP techniques – Look at the following examples and answer honestly:

If you had to choose between being with your family and having to go for an office party, which would you choose and why?

If you had to choose between a friend who never drinks and can be very boring company, and a friend who throws amazing parties, but you are sure to drink right through the night and come with a horrible hangover to work on most working days, who will you choose as your best friend?

Write down and visualize making the right choice in your mind so that when you encounter a similar real-life situation, your body and mind are prepared to choose appropriately and is duly backed by powerful reasons

Affirmations – Complete the following affirmations in your own words:

1) I am _____

2) I am undeterred by _____

3) I stand up for _____

Visualization – Remember that office situation when you had to say no to the bossy subordinate. You visualized it multiple times before you become perfect. Now, make detailed notes of that visualization and include all the elements: the words you chose, body language, gestures, tone of voice, etc.

_____
_____
_____
_____
_____
_____
_____

Workbook for the Practice of Living with Purpose

NLP techniques – Make detailed notes of at least five important goals of your life making sure they fulfill the SMART goal-setting requirement:

S – Specific
M – Measurable
A – Achievable
R – Realistic
T – Timebound

Affirmations – Create your own three affirmations that are most suited to your life goals and purposes:

1) _____
_____
_____

2) _____
_____
_____

3) _____
_____
_____

Visualization – Rate the following goals in decreasing order of importance in your life:
Having a great career
Having a happy and peaceful family life
Being extremely wealthy
Traveling the world
Pursuing your music hobby

Now, visualize success for the top three goals, and make detailed notes of that success scene. Don't worry if none of the above goals are on your list. Simply make your own goal list, rate them, and write success stories of the top three goals.

Workbook for the Practice of Personal Integrity

NLP techniques – Here are some classic examples of saying no politely. Rate them in order of your preference. Practice using them on daily. And, don't forget or hesitate to use them in real-life situations so that you can make only those promises that you can be certain of keeping:
I am really grateful to you for thinking of me; but right now my plate is really full.
Not my cup tea, thank you so much.
I am not really into gaming; but thank you for asking
I really appreciate your keenness in giving me this task, but I am excessively busy for the next couple of weeks.

Affirmations – Create three of your own affirmations most suitable for your way of living:
1)

_____

2)
_____
_____

3)
_____
_____

Maintaining a diary – Think of two of the most difficult experiences in your life when you broke a promise. Now, answer the following questions:

What were reasons for letting the concerned person down?
_____
_____
_____
_____

How did you feel about it?
_____
_____
_____
_____

What were the lessons learned from those experiences that helped improve your level of personal integrity?
_____
_____
_____
_____

Self Help For Men

Conclusion

The journey of building and developing your self-esteem definitely has a starting point, and that is the moment you choose to take action. However, there is no end-point. It is a continuous and unending learning process. As your progress on your path, you only get better than your previous state. However, there will never come the point when you can say, "I have learned everything that has to be learned in the realm of self-esteem, and there is no more room for improvement."

You must endeavor continuously to grow and build on the six crucial components of self-esteem including:
1. Living consciously
2. Self-acceptance
3. Self-responsibility
4. Self-assertiveness
5. Living with purpose
6. Personal integrity

Additionally, this book needs to be reread a couple of times and the quizzes and questionnaires repeated each time you think your level of self-esteem has gone up a few notches.

The most important element of this book is to increase self-awareness by completing the chapter-end self-assessment repeatedly.

Perhaps, the best way to end this book is with self-esteem quotes of famous and successful people. So, here goes:

Self-esteem is as important to human beings as legs are to a table. It is the foundation that supports our mental and physical happiness – Louise Hart, the hit musician from Denmark

There is overwhelming evidence that proves that the higher the level of self-esteem, the more the person will treat others respectfully, generously, and kindly – Nathaniel Branden

Part 2: Assertiveness for Men

Stop Being a Pushover and Learn to Say No by Using These Proven Techniques

+Chapter 1: Introduction to Communication Styles

What is assertiveness? It is a type of personality trait typically reflected through outward behavior and communication. A man who is assertive is one with the power to stand up for his own rights and those of others. The primary element that differentiates assertiveness from other forms of behavior and communication is the articulation of one's rights without subjugating or hurting other people in the process.

Even in the midst of an intensely conflicting argument, an assertive man will never say or do anything that offends or upsets the opposing party. In a calm and composed demeanor, he will talk about his own opinions and beliefs. Assertiveness is the perfect balance between aggression and passiveness. Therefore, assertiveness can be defined as a personality trait that empowers a man to express his opinion, beliefs, thoughts, and feelings, honestly and directly.

It is a good idea to start understanding the concept of assertiveness and how to go about building it by learning the basics about the four different primary communication styles, including:
1. Passive
2. Aggressive
3. Assertive
4. Passive-Aggressive

Passive Communication

Passive communication refers to a style in which people do not openly express their opinions, feelings, and thoughts. People with a passive communication style don't stand up and fight for their rights. They also cannot stand up for other people's rights. Typically, passive communication is associated with low self-esteem, driven by a feeling of being useless and worthless. Passive communicators are people who think that they deserve the punishments and ill-treatment they get.

Therefore, passive communicators do not react to hurtful or angry sentiments made against them. Instead of expressing their feelings, passive communicators accumulate negativities inside themselves. However, it is not possible to hold on forever. Each of us has a threshold point, and when that point is breached, the suppressed negativities burst forth in unpleasant and even dangerous ways.

Characteristics of Passive Communicators:

Bashful – Nearly all passive communicators are shy by nature and will not raise their voice to say something even if they don't like it. For example, if your boss is continuously loading you up with excess work while letting many others off, and you are not saying anything about the situation, then you are a passive communicator. Shyness prevents you from drawing attention to yourself. You simply choose to be agreeable.

Highly sensitive – Almost all passive communicators are sensitive to criticism. For example, if your boss says something like, "You must do something about your tardiness," and you take this statement to heart and feel sad and hurt, then you could have a passive communication style.

Self-conscious – Passive communicators are self-conscious of how they come across to people. This deep sense of self-consciousness is one of the primary reasons passive communicators have difficulty expressing their opinions and feelings.

All these characteristics result in depression, anxiety, and feelings of inadequacy and immaturity in passive communicators.

Examples of typical passive communicator responses and scenarios:
- I cannot say anything to my boss; I will lose my job
- I am only smart enough for this level of work; I am not worthy of a promotion
- No one loves me; I am all alone in this world
- I cannot ask that beautiful girl out for a date because I am ugly

- You visit a restaurant, and the steak you ordered is not to your satisfaction. When the waiter asks for feedback, you tell him everything is all right

Challenges faced by passive communicators:
- People will never care for your views and opinions
- You will be overlooked for promotions and bonuses
- You will be taken for granted, and unreasonable expectations will be placed on you
- Accumulation of undue stress and anxieties could lead to depression

Mao Zedong, the founding father of the People's Republic of China, said, *"Passivity is fatal. We aim to make our enemies passive!"*

Aggressive Communication

Aggressive communicators are the exact opposite of passive communicators. They voice their opinions, feelings, and thoughts so forcefully that it hurts and violates the rights of other people.

Characteristics of Aggressive Communicators:

They do not listen – Aggressive communicators rarely make an effort to listen during a conversation. Here, we are not just talking about the absence of active listening. The basic attention required to be given to someone who is talking is also missing.

Thus, aggressive listeners only project their own viewpoints, resulting in a one-way monologue instead of a healthy conversation. Moreover, if other participants do manage to voice their opinions, they are ruthlessly and forcefully rejected without rhyme or reason.

Aggressive communicators only pursue personal goals – The absence of listening during a conversation is driven by a personal agenda. Aggressive communicators typically seek just their own goals. They want only to transmit messages that meet their personal goals, and everything else is aggressively and forcefully relegated to the background. Aggressive communicators rarely speak to interact or share information with others. They only want to voice their opinion and crush the voices of everyone else in the group.

They lack empathy – The absence of listening, and the sole purpose of pursuing personal goals, combine to render aggressive communicators as totally unempathetic. All others' thoughts, feelings, and emotions are insignificant before their own.

All these characteristics make aggressive communicators come across as violent, rude, nasty, dominating, and insensitive.

Examples of typical aggressive communicator responses and scenarios:

- I am superior to you
- I am right, and you are wrong
- I will get my way, no matter what
- I can infringe upon your rights
- You owe me
- Everything is your fault

Challenges faced by aggressive communicators:
- Alienated by friends and family
- Everyone will avoid talking or interacting with them
- Despite having great oratory skills, they can never win an argument because they will never be invited for a discussion
- If they are in a position of power, then people will hate and fear them
- If they have no power, then they will be ridiculed, mocked, or worse still, completely ignored

Jose Mourinho, the famed Portuguese football manager, said, "The world today is so competitive, selfish, and aggressive that during the time we spend in this world, we must try and be everything but that."

Passive-Aggressive Communication

People with a passive-aggressive communication style are those that appear passive on the outside but are deeply aggressive on the inside. Can you think of anybody in your office whom the boss insults and humiliates? Maybe the person smiles and tries to brush off the insult, and later on tells you, in secret, that, henceforth, he is going to make life hell for his boss. That is an example of a passive-aggressive kind of behavior.

What about your dealings with your children? You are ordering them to clean their rooms, and you can hear them mutter their resentment under their breath. When you ask them to talk loudly, they simply turn around, smile, (falsely, most of the time) and say, "Nothing!" This is another classic case of passive-aggressive behavior. It is a combination of the fear of openly antagonizing authority and the deep urge to be aggressive too. They react in such a way that you cannot find a fault, and yet you know that such people are behaving in a passive-aggressive manner.

Characteristics of Passive-Aggressive Communicators:

They often use the silent treatment – The silent treatment is one of the most standard reactions used by passive-aggressive communicators. Completely ignoring someone is not really passive-aggressive, as it is an explicit behavior. For example, there could be a coworker who 'accidentally' doesn't see you in the hallway when you greet him. When you remind him, he simply says he didn't see.

They use subtle insults – For example, a colleague could say something nice to you in front of others, for which you might even thank him. However, when you think about it later, you realize that the compliment was an insult in disguise.

Sulking behavior – Sulking and being grumpy are typical of teenage passive-aggressive behavior. You refuse to give your son permission for a night out with his friends. Sulking, being grumpy, not sitting at the table to have dinner with the rest of the family, etc., are classic cases of passive-aggressive behavior.

Vengeful – A passive-aggressive person will not forget the pain and agony of not having the strength to fight back, so he chooses to find deceptive ways of taking revenge. For example, it is possible that a resentful subordinate will secretly go behind your back to your boss to complain about you.

Examples of typical passive-aggressive communicator responses and scenarios:
- *I am not mad* – This is, perhaps, the most common response from a passive-aggressive communicator. Even when directly asked to express his feelings, this person will not, and instead will seethe within himself.
- *Fine! Whatever!* – Classic phrases of sulking behavior
- *I am coming* – Verbally, they will be heeding orders, but they will use every delay tactic to put off implementing the orders
- *You always find a fault with me* – A typical response by teenage children when asked to clean the room or improve their grades

Challenges of passive-aggressive behavior
- Such individuals remain stuck with their negative emotions; in fact, such people are at a higher risk of becoming depressed because the accumulation of negative energy stem from two sources; from being aggressive and from being passive
- They might resolve their immediate resentment through underhanded means, but the root problem remains unresolved
- Passive-aggressive people's true personalities come out sooner, rather than later, and they become alienated from people

Assertive Communication

An assertive communication style is one that helps you balance the passive and aggressive styles. An assertive person will state his feelings, thoughts, and opinions firmly, but without violating the rights and beliefs of other people. Abraham Lincoln said, *"Those who deny freedom to others do not deserve it themselves."* Therefore, an assertive man is one who will say what he wants to say and allow others to state their opinions too.

Characteristics of Assertive Communicators:

Respectful behavior – Assertive people respect everyone involved in a conversation and value all comments and remarks

Sincere interaction – Unlike passive-aggressive communicators, whose outer behavior does not align with their inner personality, assertive communicators say what they feel, without any pretense.

Value and accept themselves – This approach gives assertive people self-confidence that is rooted in self-awareness and not in arrogance. They accept themselves for their strengths and weaknesses.

Excellent emotional stability and self-control – Assertive people know how to manage their emotions, which helps them handle the most intense arguments, calmly and composedly.

Excellent communication skills – Assertive people work on their communication skills and are always working to develop and improve them. They understand the importance of communication for great interpersonal relationships and success.

Examples of typical assertive communicator responses and scenarios:

- I am confident of myself, but I also know you could be right in your perspective
- We are all entitled to our views, opinions, and thoughts
- I speak with honesty and clarity
- I get straight to the point and avoid beating around the bush
- I value my personal rights and will not let anyone violate them. I also respect and honor the individual rights of others.

Benefits of assertive communication:

- You will earn the respect of your colleagues, boss, and coworkers
- Your family will also love and respect you for what you are
- As you will be focused on addressing core issues in your life, you will mature and develop as a human being
- You will be quite popular and well-liked by most people because of your ability to respect everyone

Generally, women are considered to be less assertive than men, although this trend is changing radically in the modern world. This outlook actually puts more pressure on men because they are expected to already be in possession of this skill. Irrespective of your level of assertiveness, the good thing is that you can improve on it and get better at it through diligent practice and hard work. The art of assertiveness will give you a big edge in this rather competitive world.

Chapter 2:
Why Do We Behave the Way We Do?

The idea of aggressive and passive-aggressive behaviors in modern times is not very difficult to explain and understand. There is a lot of pressure in the modern world to behave appropriately and not let emotions overtake and overwhelm us. Therefore, even as children, we are taught to suppress emotions, especially negative ones, so that we look "dignified" and "civilized." Many of us are trained to believe that suppressing emotions is the most effective way of handling them.

However, that is not really true. Our emotions work in tandem with our intelligence to help us understand the world and its happenings. Emotions orchestrate our lives. Sometimes, the resultant music can be a sad and depressing tune, while, at other times, it may be happy and refreshing.

An old Arab proverb goes something like this: "A man who cannot understand the look can never comprehend the explanation." Emotions speak a universal language and bind human beings together. It is unfortunate that such a beautiful element of human beings is being suppressed instead of being used effectively.

Moreover, emotions are nothing but energy that helps us manage the ups and downs in our lives. Suppressing emotions is equivalent to locking up the energy inside our system. The more we suppress our emotions, the more they accumulate in our body and mind. This accumulation of energy is called the "percolator effect."

Percolators are used to make coffee. You put in the coffee powder, add some water, and switch on the machine. The energy from the coffee is released and accumulates inside the percolator, allowing the coffee to brew perfectly. If you don't let the steam from the machine out at the right time, it will burst forth, spewing hot coffee all over you.

Similarly, our emotions are being "brewed" inside our body, and we need to find suitable exits for the emotions so that our lives turn out as perfectly-balanced coffee, poured from a well-maintained percolator. Mature expressions of emotions are the healthiest way of releasing them from our systems. Instead, if we suppress and accumulate them, they will burst forth when the threshold of repressed emotions is breached, ending up spewing venom all around. The result of repressed emotions can be devastating for everyone involved.

Aggressive people use violent and nasty ways to express their emotions while passive-aggressive people use underhanded ways of dealing with their emotions. Both these methods are not only ineffective ways of releasing emotional energy from our system but also have harmful and dangerous consequences, as discussed in Chapter 1.

Reasons for Aggressive Behavior in Men

Identifying the underlying causes of aggressive behavior will help you manage your communication style better than before. There are some scientifically proven reasons for aggressive behavior in men:

The brain of a man is not wired for empathy – Multiple research studies have revealed that the male brain is not really wired for empathy. It is more wired for problem-solving than trying to listen to and relate to underlying emotions. This is one of the reasons why your wife is constantly complaining that you don't listen to her problems. The instant she starts complaining, your brain is hardwired to find solutions for her, and all she wants is for you to listen to her. Stopping her in midsentence is the most primal and basic form of aggression.

Men have higher levels of testosterone – Higher levels of testosterone are directly connected to aggressive and violent behavior. While genetic factors play a role in the amount of testosterone in your system, the social and physical conditions around you also play a critical role. When your life is strengthened through strong familial bonds, and you surround yourself with loving friends and family, then your testosterone levels decrease, thereby lowering your urge for aggression.

Men have lower levels of oxytocin – Studies have

revealed that people with higher levels of oxytocin are friendlier, more trusting, more empathetic, and less aggressive than people with lower levels of oxytocin, a chemical that is naturally produced in our body. Oxytocin generates a feeling of empathy, resulting in gentle behavior. Additionally, testosterone is known to block the functioning of oxytocin.

The good thing for men is that it is relatively straightforward to raise oxytocin levels. Regular massages are known to increase oxytocin levels. You could also make a conscious effort to trust other people instead of being fearful and defensive.

Unresolved childhood problems such as trauma, abuse, and more – The sudden death of a loved one, parents who were always fighting with each other, or physical, sexual, or emotional abuse during childhood are personality-affecting incidences. If these issues remain unresolved, then their negative impacts in adulthood will result in aggressive behavior.

Low self-esteem – One of the most significant contributing factors to aggressive behavior is low self-esteem. Men who feel unworthy and unloved use aggressive behaviors to cover up their inner feelings.

Reasons for Passive-Aggressive Behavior in Men

The only difference between aggressive and passive-aggressive behavior is in the manifestation of the aggression. Aggressive men tend to openly resist authority or use discernible ways to show their aggression. Passive-aggressive men, on the other hand, choose more subtle ways of showing their aggression. Here are some reasons why some men choose passive-aggression over aggression:

Showing negative emotions is not socially acceptable – Modern society treats displays of anger with disdain. As already mentioned earlier, we are trained to suppress emotions, rather than show or express them. Expressing emotions maturely is a sign of assertiveness, a quality that non-assertive men lack. Therefore, to appear compliant with accepted social norms, they tend to act in a passive-aggressive way.

It is easy to get away with passive-aggressive behaviors – Passive-aggressive behaviors ride on the thin line separating the two extremes between passivity and aggression. So, bad behavior in passive-aggressive men is difficult to differentiate from open aggression which helps them get away with it.

For example, if your boss tells you to do something, and you whisper your resentment under your breath instead of openly being aggressive, then that is showing passive-aggression. When your boss, who knows you've said something, challenges you to speak your thoughts, you can choose to say, "Nothing, boss!" Easy to get away with.

Getting revenge is one of the most wonderful things to happen – Passive-aggressive people are typically out to get revenge for their humiliation or feelings of being insulted. In fact, aggressive people really don't care about revenge because they have already managed to strangle other people's opinions and views while forcefully presenting their own ideas. Aggressive people do end up expressing their feelings, even if wrongly and damagingly.

On the other hand, passive-aggressive people are not able to express their emotions, openly resulting in vengefulness. For example, your boss asks you to do a presentation that you don't really want to do. You swear under your breath, put on a false smile for him, and grudgingly take on the task.

The way to get revenge is to do a shoddy job with your presentation. You have followed your boss' orders outwardly, but he knows, and you know that shoddy work requires him to redo the entire thing. And he cannot even be angry because you can say that you did what you believed you thought was right. Perfect and classic example of passive-aggressive behavior!

Passive-aggressive behavior gives you the satisfaction (even if only cursory) of expressing your resentment or anger without the responsibility of the consequences that come with aggressive behavior. In many ways, passive-aggressive behaviors are more dangerous and unpleasant than aggressive behaviors. In the latter, there is at least a sense of openness involved, with little or no guile.

Examples of Famous People Who Did Not Need Aggression

One of the most common reasons given by men for their aggression is that they believe they require this trait to be successful. Such men believe that leaders and famous people are seen to be loud, needlessly emphatic, and aggressive. Nothing is farther from the truth than this concept. Here are some examples of famous people and great leaders who never need aggression to achieve success:

Tom Hanks – This Hollywood superstar who could, perhaps, get away with aggressive behavior, thanks to his overwhelming global popularity, is a super-nice man who chooses to typewrite responses to every fan letter on beautiful stationery. He treats every opinion and feedback with dignity and honor.

Sigmund Freud – The father of psychoanalysis did not only treat famous and rich people. A distraught mother of a gay individual wrote to him, begging him to "cure" her son of homosexuality. This happened when a large portion of the American population was blaming the gay community for causing the Great Depression. The letter he wrote to this lady was way ahead of its time when he explained the naturalness of her son's state of mind.

The detailed letter reflects Sigmund Freud's painstaking efforts to understand the lady's and her son's pain and help them overcome it. Another great example of how great men do not need aggression to become popular and famous.

Stan Lee of Marvel Comics – Today, Stan Lee is nothing short of being a god to comic lovers across the globe. However, way back in 1947, he was still a novice in the industry and was working as a junior editor with *Timely Comics*, the precursor to *Marvel Comics*. During that time, he wrote a little book called *Secrets Behind the Comics* in which he promised to edit and review any reader's aspiring work of comic art for a sum of $1.

Now, cut to 1972. Russell Maheras was a budding comic artist, while Stan Lee had grown by leaps and bounds in his career and was the editor-in-chief of Marvel Comics. Russell Maheras had a copy of Stan Lee's 1947 book. He sent a copy of his comic art, which he called *Superman*, along with the required dollar amount, to Stan Lee for his review, reminding him of the promise he'd made to all his readers way back in 1947.

And true to his word (despite having the luxury of getting away without heeding the request), Stan Lee sent back a detailed editor's note to Russell Maheras, praising him highly for certain elements and critiquing him for others! An assertive, promise-delivering gentleman to the core!

If you are an aggressive or passive-aggressive person, and you are slowly but surely realizing the disadvantages and futility of such behaviors, then you don't need to fret. The desire to change is the first and most important step in a positive direction. With tips, suggestions, and recommendations from this book, you can easily turn over a new leaf to build and develop assertiveness.

Chapter 3:
Current Level of Assertiveness

'When I discover who I am, I'll be free," said Ralph Ellison, one of America's most influential scholar, literary critic, and novelist.

This chapter is dedicated to helping you become self-aware; to help you understand how assertive you are right now. The questions are based on the self-expression scale taken from *The College Self-Expression Scale*, published by John P. Galassi and others in 1974.

The questions are phrased to elicit a "Yes" or "No" answer from you. In the end, count the number of "yesses" and "nos." The "yesses" reflect your assertiveness and the "nos" reflect the lack thereof.

Questionnaire #1 to Identify Your Current Level of Assertiveness

Q1. Suppose you are standing in line at a bank which has four people in front of you and three more after you.

Another man walks in, skips the line, and goes straight to the teller to get his work done. He does not even glance at the people waiting in line. Will you tell this man to go back and take his rightful place at the end of the line? Y/N

Q2. You buy your wife a lovely new dress from a shopping mall, located some distance away from your home. The person who serves you promises that everything is all right with the dress and that she has checked it. Your wife, however, finds a little tear near the sleeve. Will you go back to the store, register a complaint, and get an exchange? Y/N

Q3. You and your colleague have a big argument about a joint presentation you have to prepare for the CFO's visit in 10 days' time. The argument is about how to make it most effective. You have a viewpoint, and your colleague has something entirely different. You win the battle, and the first draft of the presentation (which took up three days of work) is completed and taken to your boss for approval. He takes one look at it and disapproves of it immediately. He further explains how the presentation should be done, which is exactly what your colleague was talking about. Will you accept your mistake and apologize to your colleague? Y/N

Q4. If you are angry with your children or your wife, do you express your anger in a straightforward and upfront manner, supporting your emotion with suitable reasons? Y/N

Q5. Your best friend of many years has been borrowing small amounts of money from you lately, without returning it most of the time. This time he has asked for a relatively large amount of money. Will you turn him down, citing honest reasons regarding his lack of intention to repay the amounts borrowed earlier? Y/N

Q6. In any group conversation, do you take care to draw out quiet people and ensure that you listen to and honor everyone's point of view and opinions? Y/N

Q7. In group conversations, do you make an effort to voice your opinions and views firmly, but take care not to hurt or violate other people's rights? Y/N

Q8. Are you comfortable openly asking for favors from your friend(s)?

Q9. You have finally gotten this beautiful hot girl from your office to go on a date with you. You have chosen a fairly pricey, high-end restaurant for your dinner. You are leaving no stone unturned to show your date how sophisticated and suave you are. Your dinner arrives, and the steak is not cooked the way you asked for it. Although your date has asked for the same thing, she doesn't seem too upset about her food. Will you call the waiter and express your disappointment? Y/N

Q10. You are planning to accessorize your new car but need to be under a strict budget. The salesman at the accessory shop is showing you fabulous add-ons for your car which are way above your budget. Will you be able to say no to the salesman and stick to the most basic accessories within your budget? Y/N

Q11. Your teenage child is studying for his upcoming SAT exams next week. It's a weekend and a few of your friends arrive, unannounced, to spend the day with you. They are great friends. But the noise of all of you guys together is definitely going to disturb your son. Will you politely tell your friends to go away now and choose another more convenient day for the day-long party? Y/N

Q12. Are you comfortable sharing your views and opinions with your friends and family members? Y/N

Q13. Are you comfortable sharing your views and opinions with your office colleagues and the people in your professional circle? Y/N

Q14. You are in the middle of a meeting in which your boss is making a presentation. Suddenly he says something that you know to be incorrect. Your boss' boss is also present in the meeting. Will you stand up and correct him? Y/N

Q15. An old and respected ex-boss visits you for dinner. You owe this man a lot because he taught you the tricks of the trade when you started in the profession. Now he says something that you strongly disagree with. Will you politely say so and offer a counterpoint? Y/N

Q16. You go to the local hardware store to buy some nails. You take the change, without counting it, and walk out. On the way home, you notice that you have been short-changed. Will you walk back and request the correct change? Y/N

Q17. An old buddy who has helped you many times before

with loans of money now comes to you with an unreasonable, even immoral, request. Will you stand up to him and say no? Y/N

Q18. Your favorite sister, who is going through a terrible divorce, wants to take up residence in your house which is already quite small for the four of you, including your wife and two kids. Will you tell her so and help her find other accommodation? Y/N

Q19. You are playing a baseball game with some boys in the neighborhood. It's a team of adults vs. kids. Nearly all the adults are professional players, including you. The kids are not professionals. But they are young, energetic, and quick to learn. They seem to be winning the game. You notice a close friend indulging in some underhanded dealing which results in your team winning the game. Will you stand up and question your friend? Y/N

Q20. You are going steady with a girl, and it almost seems that both of you might get married. Wanting to be upfront with her, you choose to tell her some closely-guarded secrets, including some embarrassing ones involving your friends. She goes around spreading what she has heard from you, and everyone in the neighborhood has a good laugh at you and your friends. Will you raise your voice against this betrayal and leave your girlfriend? Y/N

Q21. You are waiting in a line at one of the cash counters in a department store when you notice the billing clerk attending to someone who was not standing in the line. Will you go to the store manager and complain? Y/N

Q22. When you are in dire straits, do you feel comfortable taking financial help from friends and family? Y/N

Q23. Most of the time, you can laugh at yourself. However, today, there is this one colleague who is mocking you far more than normal, despite you telling her that she has crossed the line of decency. Will you stand up and voice your resentment? Y/N

Q24. You have arrived late for an important office meeting which has already begun. Will you walk up to the front row and take your seat without feeling uncomfortable? Remember, you also have the option of sitting inconspicuously in any of the last rows. Y/N

Q25. You are discussing an important upcoming project with your team member and your boss walks in, demanding that he speak to you immediately. Will you politely tell him that you will go to his office after finishing the ongoing project discussion with your team member? Y/N

Q26. Are comfortable being assertive? Y/N

Questionnaire #2 to Identify Your Current Level of Assertiveness

Choose the appropriate answer from the options given to each of the following questions:

Q1. Someone aggressively moves ahead of you while you are standing patiently in line. What do you do?
1. Give the person the benefit of the doubt and gently

tell him that there is a line to be followed
2. Look at him angrily but say nothing. Instead, push him "accidentally" and take your rightful place
3. Do or say nothing
4. In a firm tone, tell the person to go back to his correct place in the line

Q2. Your friend is coming over to work on an office project over the weekend. He is supposed to be there by 9:00 a.m., but he only comes in at 10:00. What will you do?
1. Be rude with him and tell him you don't like this kind of undisciplined behavior
2. Keep quiet about the whole thing because you don't like conflicts
3. Ask him politely for the reason for his delay and let him know not to repeat it again
4. You leave the house at 9:30 so that he doesn't find you when he arrives

Assertiveness Journal to Know Your Current Status

Another great way to find your current level of assertiveness is by maintaining a journal. For about a fortnight to a month, maintain a journal in which you write down daily experiences and encounters where you were assertive and not so assertiveness.

- Did you say what you wanted to say?
- What was your communication style?
- What were the feelings going on in your mind?
- Did you manage your emotions without allowing them to overwhelm you?

- Was the outcome of the event directly affected by your ability/inability to handle your emotions?
- Can you identify areas in which you could have behaved in a different way to achieve a better result? What are these areas, and how you could have done better?

When you're making these entries in your journal, remember not to judge yourself. After all, the event is over and done with. You are only looking at learning critical lessons. Have an objective outlook and make detailed notes in your journal on a daily basis.

Use the three tools given in this chapter to correctly gauge your current level of assertiveness and any necessary areas of improvement. You can start working on your self-assertiveness skills from that point.

Chapter 4:
Building Assertiveness Based On Your Core Values

Mahatma Gandhi said, "Your beliefs become your thoughts. Your thoughts become your words. Your words become your actions. Your actions become your habits. Your habits become your values. Your values become your destiny."

What is the meaning of core values and what is their importance in one's life? We will start this chapter by answering these questions before moving on to how to identify your core values. What are core values? They are personal qualities or traits that guide us in our path to our goals. Core values are ideas that enhance the worth of our lives and give them a solid structure.

When we don't have core values, we end up simply drifting through our lives in the direction we are pulled. The best part is that we can define our own core values depending on our personality makeup, our upbringing, our culture, our future goals, and more. What is the importance of defining core values?

Importance of Core Values

Core values give us a sense of purpose – Core values act as an inner compass for our life choices. They help us make decisions based on our own needs instead of drifting along our life path based on external factors such as social and situational pressures. Without core values, we lead our lives to fulfill the needs of others instead of our own. Core values help us lead our own lives instead of living someone else's. Therefore, these values give us a sense of direction and purpose which, in turn, results in happiness.

Core values facilitate making the right choices – Well-defined core values help us make the right choices in our life. Without core values, we could end up making choices that directly conflict with our needs. Moreover, making choices becomes simpler than before because we have only to follow our internal compass. When we are faced with a dilemma, all we need to do is opt for the choice that is aligned with our core values.

Core values make us confident – When we have something of value to guide our lives, we are filled with confidence. Core values give us courage and confidence to lead our lives in the "right" way.

Discovering and Defining Core Values

There are over 400 core values from which you can choose

the ones that you want to define your life's path. Some of them include spirituality, independence, humor, growth, happiness, power, progress, self-reliance, success, forgiveness, and many, many more.

However, instead of choosing from an arbitrary list, it is best to choose from those traits that are already deeply ingrained in our systems. These traits are the ones that we have unwittingly used or not used to make our earlier life choices.

This exercise of discovering and identifying your core values will take a little bit of time and energy, especially if you are doing it for the first time. But it's definitely worth the effort because the outcome of the exercise will be useful throughout your life.

Step 1: Recall the best 4-5 experiences in your life – Reflect on the various events that have happened in your life. Get information from your diary if you have maintained one. Otherwise, simply sit back and jog your memory and think of the top four or five experiences that have given you immense happiness and pleasure. Answer the following questions based on those chosen life experiences:

- What happened? Describe it in detail.
- What were the emotions you felt?
- What were your thoughts?
- Write down the list of personal values that you expressed during the experience. And write down how these values affected your experience

You might have started this exercise with self-doubt,

thinking, "how will I remember what happened many years ago?" However, you will realize that many of those happy moments are deeply ensconced in your psyche. When you jog your memory a little bit, you can relive almost the entire experience, especially the emotional memories. Moreover, the values that enhanced the joy of the experience will stand out in your memory.

Step 2: Recall the worst 4-5 life experiences – These memories are typically easy to retrieve because painful memories are more deeply entrenched in our minds than joyful ones. Answer the same set of questions as you did for your best experiences. Only, this time, the last question will be replaced with, "Write down the list of personal values that you were suppressing during the experience. And write down how these values affected your experience."

Step 3: Identify your code of conduct – To arrive at this, you must identify those elements that enhance the value in your life experiences. Think of those elements that come immediately after basic survival needs of food, clothing, and shelter. These items must be so important to you that, without them, your life will have no meaning whatsoever. In the absence of these elements, you might not die, but you will also not thrive. Examples are:

- A state of continuous learning
- Adventure and thrill
- Financial security
- Family happiness
- Work-life balance
- Good health

- The beauty of nature

Step 4: Group similar values together – Group together similar values from the list you created by following the above three steps. For example, responsibility, timeliness, and discipline can all be grouped together. Similarly, spirituality, prayers, God, and wisdom can be grouped together.

Step 5: Identify the central theme of each group of values – For example, responsibility, timeliness, and discipline could be categorized as "discipline," and the common theme that runs through spirituality, prayers, God, and wisdom is "spirituality."

Step 6 – Make your final list – The number of core values in the final list should ideally be somewhere between five and 10, give or take a few. This number is important to bear in mind while creating your personal list of core values because less than five might not cover all the elements for a meaningful and fulfilling life and more than 10 might be difficult to manage and keep track of.

Step 7 – Rank your final list of core values – This last step in the somewhat big exercise of creating a personal list of core values is bound to take a little more time than you think. Ranking seemingly equally important list of values can be quite a challenge.

First, rank them as per your gut feel. Sleep on it, and look at the list again the next morning. If your ranking seems fine, then you are most likely on the right path. However, if it feels wrong, then redo the ranking. Repeat until you are satisfied with your list. The ranking is necessary for those occasions when you are in a dilemma that includes two or more values from your own list. At such times, the ranking system gives you amazing clarity on the priorities involved in the dilemma.

Core Values and Assertiveness

Once you have your core values in place and are completely engaged with them, your ability to enhance your level of assertiveness will go up a few notches. While communication is one of the most evident forms of assertiveness, this trait includes a lot more than communication.

Assertiveness is all about core values. In its most wholesome form, assertiveness is a way of life that gives us the power and freedom to live according to our values and principles and not someone else's.

Assertiveness is about accepting ourselves the way we are, including our weaknesses, without feelings of shame or guilt. In addition to communicating effectively, assertiveness includes:

Keeping our promises – Not keeping our word, or flaking out on our commitments, dents our self-confidence, leading to reduced levels of assertiveness that are driven by low levels of certainty. Core values help you make only those promises that are important in your life; this is an attitude that renders certainty, and therefore self-confidence and assertiveness.

No need to second-guess our choices – A well-drafted core values list, based on increased self-awareness through self-questioning, will ensure that we never have to second-guess our choices, empowering us to be assertive at all times.

Commitment to achieving our goals – Goals are nothing but promises you have made to yourself. So, like keeping your word when you promise something to others, assertiveness helps you keep the promises you make to yourself. Core values play an important role throughout the journey of your goals, right from the time of goal-setting up to their realization.

Defending our beliefs – Being assertive also means standing up for our rights and beliefs if they are in danger of being violated. Core values help us understand and articulate our beliefs, thereby helping us have an increased level of assertiveness.

Therefore, identifying and crystallizing your core values is, perhaps, the first step to increase assertiveness.

Chapter 5:
Change Your Inner Beliefs

Our thinking process, and the conditioning of our minds, is dependent on our inner beliefs. And most of our inner beliefs are already deeply ensconced in our psyche. An important element in your journey to increase your assertiveness is to change your inner beliefs and thought processes. As a grown man, you already have preconceived notions about most of the things and people around you, and about yourself too.

Many of our beliefs are carried forward from our childhood, when we were taught certain things. It requires a change in mindset to bring about tangible changes within yourself and the world. For example, until Barack Obama changed his inner belief that an African-American could never become the president of the United States of America and followed through with his goals and visions, all of us believed similarly.

Another classic example of preconditioned inner beliefs is the misconception that outward expressions of anger and sadness are forbidden. Now, as an adult, you know that there are mature ways of assertively expressing anger and sadness. Therefore, this old inner belief is wrong, and you need to change it to live a more meaningful life than before.

Similarly, we must let go and change all those old inner beliefs that have no value today. Here are some more inner beliefs that drive unassertive thinking:

• I must not express my negative emotions because it is wrong to burden others with my problems
• Asserting my ideas and opinions might hurt the other person, and my relationship with that individual will be ruined
• It is embarrassing to speak about my beliefs and thoughts
• If someone has said "no" to my request for help, then it means that the concerned person does not like or love me
• I do not have to talk about my inner feelings; the people who are really close to me and understand me should be able to read them
• It is selfish to say whatever I want
• Neither I, nor anyone else, has a right to change their mind
• Ideally, people should keep their emotions to themselves
• If I talk about my nervousness and fear, people will think I am weak and mock me
• If I take praise from others, it means I am arrogant

Assertive Rights

Assertive rights were first published in the 1975 book, *When I say No, I feel Guilty,* written by Manuel J. Smith. He proposed a "bill of assertive rights" which every human being should have. Some of those rights include:

• Everyone, including you, has a right to judge his or her own behavior, emotions, and thoughts and take self-responsibility for the consequences.

• Everyone has a right to say "no"

• No one needs to offer excuses or reasons to justify his or her behavior

• You can judge other people's behavior only if you are responsible for finding solutions to their problems

• Everyone has a right to change his or her mind

• Everyone has a right to disagree with anyone's opinion

• Everyone has the right to make mistakes and accept responsibility for mistakes

• Everyone has the right to say, "I don't know."

• Everyone has the right to be illogical while making choices

• Everyone has the right to say, "I don't understand."

• Everyone has the right to say, "I don't care."

Changing Your Inner Beliefs

So you have to move from unassertive thinking to assertive thinking, and that starts with changing your inner beliefs. But how to go about altering your inner beliefs? The first step to that is to assess your current inner beliefs. Some people might be able to change their way of thinking and their inner beliefs simply by knowing and accepting the assertive right that they have a right to make changes.

However, for some others, this simple technique might not work. They need to challenge their existing inner beliefs head-on, a process called disputation. Disputation is a psychological method of making changes and is based on the idea that our current inner beliefs are primarily learned opinions and not facts. Opinions can be challenged and questioned and need not be blindly followed, especially if they are harming us.

To dispute your thoughts, you need to get to their roots and find evidence for and against those views. Maintaining thought diaries is an effective way to gauge your current beliefs, and then to go about changing them for your own good.

Maintaining thought diaries – The thoughts that run in our minds are random and erratic, and keeping track of them is a huge challenge. Making notes of our thoughts is one of the most effective ways of recalling our thoughts when we need them. Maintaining thought diaries of all your unassertive thoughts will give you a good insight into your current status of inner beliefs.

To make sample entries in your thought diary, let us take an example of a typical friendship scenario. You and your best friends are team leaders managing two different teams within the same department. Both the teams have often helped each other during work overload.

Now, on a particularly difficult day with multiple deadlines hitting your team, you ask your best friend to help. However, he says no. You feel bad about the entire thing and somehow get through the day. You go home and make journal entries in your thought diary.

Part I of the thought diary involves making journal entries regarding your emotions, behavior, and thoughts:

Identifying your emotions – Delve deep into your mind and find answers to the following questions:
What were your feelings? Hurt? Anger? Disbelief? Also rate the intensity of your feelings using numbers 1-10, where 1 stands for least intense and 10 stands for most intense.

_____
_____
_____
_____
_____

Identifying your thoughts – The situation was quite intense. You were already burdened by overwork, and your best friend refused to help. What were the thoughts running through your head?
What were your thoughts? Also rate the intensity of your thoughts using numbers 1-10, where 1 stands for least intense and 10 stands for most intense.

_____
_____
_____
_____
_____

Identifying your behavior – In this intense situation, how did you behave?

What were your physical sensations? What did you do? How did you react/respond? Also rate the intensity of your thoughts using numbers 1-10, where 1 stands for least intense and 10 stands for most intense.

_____
_____
_____
_____
_____

Here are some basic rules to follow when you answer the self-questions on your emotions, thoughts, and behavior:
- Stick only to the facts.
- Don't include your opinions and interpretations. For example, an entry like, "My best friend rudely refused to help me today," is your interpretation. "When I requested help, my friend say no" is factual.
- The rates of intensity of the emotion, thought, or behavior reflect the strength of your inner belief; the higher the rating you gave, the stronger the inner belief that drives that emotion, thought, or behavior.

Part II of the thought diary – This part has your answers to the following self-responses:
- How can I categorize my behavior? Was I aggressive, passive, passive-aggressive, or assertive?
- Can I identify any evidence for my emotions, thoughts, and behaviors? If yes, what was the evidence?
- Was I ignoring either one of our assertive rights during the event?
- What other perspectives was I missing in the situation?

Here are some sample answers for the two parts of the thought diary of the illustrative experience:

Part I of the thought diary would typically have the following answers:

What were your feelings? *I felt anger and hurt.*
Rate the intensity – *Anger – 8, Hurt – 8*
What were your thoughts? *How could my best friend do this to me? How many times have I helped him, even when I knew I was stretching my team members? How will I meet my deadlines for the day? I always help him whenever he asks.*

Intensity rate - *How could my best friend do this to me? – 9 How will I meet my deadlines for the day? – 8 I always help him whenever he asks – 9*
What were your physical sensations? What did you do? How did you react/respond? – *I did not speak to my friend the entire day after that. When he called me to join him for an evening drink after office hours, I said no.*

Part II of the thought diary would typically have the following entries:

How can I categorize my behavior? Was I aggressive, passive, passive-aggressive, or assertive? *I was passive-aggressive because I chose to ignore him, instead of openly asking him for the reason for his refusal to help.*

Can I identify any evidence for my emotions, thoughts, and behaviors? If yes, what was the evidence? *No, there is no evidence of any kind*

Was I ignoring either one of our assertive rights during the event? *Yes, I was ignoring my right to say no when I chose to help him even when I knew I could not. I was ignoring the rights of my team members when I overworked them for my best friend. By being angry with my friend, I was ignoring his rights to say no.*

What other perspectives was I missing in the situation? *The perspectives that I could have missed in my state of high emotion include:*
• My friend's team may already have been overworked
• He might have had a significantly strong and understandable reason to have had to refuse to help me
• There are multiple occasions when I have also said no to him
• I could have thought that this one experience can hardly create a dent in our friendship

How could I have had a more assertive kind of response to the same situation? I could have asked him the reason for his negative response, then and there, instead of sulking.

Now, if you rate the intensity of your emotions and thoughts, you will notice a significant drop. Primarily, you are training your mind not to react and respond based on emotions. You are attempting to change your inner belief that emotions should drive behavior to the idea that objective thinking should drive behavior.

Make multiple entries like this in your thought diary, and keep increasing self-awareness and making changes to your inner beliefs with each lesson.

Chapter 6: Communication Techniques to Practice

Winston Churchill said, "Success is not final and failure is not fatal. What matters is the courage to persist and having the right attitude." You see the power of his communication technique. Just the right words with outstanding impact!

To be able to improve your assertiveness skills in communication, it makes sense to first understand what factors affect the way you communicate.

Reasons for passive communication:
- Overly focused on pleasing everyone except themselves
- Insufficient levels of self-confidence
- Overly anxious about whether their opinions and views will be unacceptable to others
- Intensely sensitive to criticism
- Not building assertive communication skills
- Reasons for aggressive communication:

- Overly focused on achieving one's own desires and needs
- Overconfidence
- Not learning to respect and regard others' opinions and views
- Poor listening skills

Reasons for assertive communication:

Well-developed self-confidence, without arrogance

High level of self-awareness including strengths and weaknesses

Acceptance of who they are

Resilience to criticism and negative feedback

Always in self-improvement mode

Tips to Improve Assertiveness in Your Communication

Say "no" more often – Here are some commonly used assertive responses and phrases that work in many situations. You can learn some of them by rote and use them whenever you have to say no assertively:

- I really appreciate your efforts, but I am not interested at all
- Thanks for the offer, but I cannot make time for this now
- Thanks for your help, but I want to do this on my own
- Thank you very much, but definitely a no (don't forget to smile genuinely with this response)
- Thanks a lot for considering me to be part of your great team, but I'm afraid I will have to pass up the offer this time around.

- Thanks a lot for reaching out to me, but I'm afraid I have a far more important element going on in my life that requires my undivided focus.
- Thank you for your opinion; what do the others in the group think?
- That seems like a good idea. Can I take a couple of weeks to think about it?
- What you're telling me sounds like an urgent request. However, I will not be able to give it that kind of attention right now.
- I don't appreciate your tone of voice (or use of bad language or choice of words)
- Can you please respect and have regard for my perspective too?
- I felt offended by your behavior
- I understand your love for adventure, but it is not my cup of tea

Practice the right tone of voice – An assertive tone of voice is powerful, strong, and yet calm and friendly. Have you watched Al Pacino in *The Godfather*? Even in the most violent of scenes, his tone of voice rings of assertiveness and not aggression! Or for that matter, listen to Morgan Freeman's voice and you can distinctly hear an authoritative ring, cushioned beautifully with a calm demeanor.

You must practice talking aloud to yourself using different tones of voices and see which sounds the best. Your calmness should come from within, which means you must "feel" calm. Here are some tips to improve your tone of voice:

Step 1: Identify those situations when your tone of voice is not natural. Here are a few prompts for you to recall experiences and remember if your voice was "off" during the interaction:

- How comfortable are you in a business meeting setting?
- Are you comfortable sharing your thoughts and ideas in team meetings?
- Do your colleagues respond positively to your ideas when you speak out?
- Are you comfortable talking to your family members? Feel free to break this question up further and ask yourself how comfortable you are talking to your parents, spouse, kids, elders in the family, cousins, siblings, etc.
- Are you comfortable talking to strangers you meet in public places?

Recall your tone of voice in each of these experiences and make a note of those situations when you think it was not right. These are the situations you are uncomfortable in, and so your tone of voice sounds off."

Step 2: Find your casual tone of voice. It is that voice you use to ask someone at your dinner table to pass the salt or pepper. It is your most natural voice. You don't raise your voice, and yet are loud enough for your dining companion to hear you.

This natural tone of voice is best suited for assertive communication. It is the tone of voice you must use in all situations including your interaction with your wife, parents, coworker, subordinates, and your boss.

Step 3: This "pass the salt" tone of voice is what you need to use in all your uncomfortable situations as well. Recall those uncomfortable situations from Step 1 and, this time, imagine yourself using the "pass the salt" natural tone of voice in each of the situations.

It will take some amount of practice to get over the discomfort of using your natural tone of voice even during uncomfortable situations. Keep rehearsing the uncomfortable situations, speaking aloud to yourself using your natural tone of voice. Initially, speaking emotion-laden words in a natural tone of voice might seem weird. But, with practice, you will realize how much more impactfully assertive your voice sounds when you use your natural tone.

Step 4: Don't hesitate to practice the natural tone in the real-world too. Rehearsing on your own is quite different from speaking in the outside world. So use the first opportunity you get to speak like this in a real scenario. Try it with someone you trust, such as your spouse or your kids or a sibling who is close to you.

Alternately, you can try this "pass the salt" with strangers or billing clerks or a salesperson in a shop. Focus on verbalizing every word deliberately, which will increase the clarity of your speech. With regular practice, you will find yourself habituated into using a natural tone of voice that makes you sound assertive and confident.

Practice listening skills – Assertiveness calls for

increased sensitivity to other people's views, opinions, and thoughts. Excellent listening skills are essential for understanding and appreciating others' perspectives. Here are some tips to improve your listening skills and become more assertive than before:

Tip #1: Maintain healthy eye contact with the speaker. Ensure you give your entire attention to the conversation. Working on your computer or looking at your mobile phone while someone is speaking to you is a typical reaction of an aggressive person (if the speaker is your subordinate) or passive-aggressive style (if the speaker holds a higher position than you). Avoid this completely, and maintain eye contact with the speaker throughout the conversation.

Tip #2: Practice paying attention to the speaker without appearing overbearing or anxious. Sometimes when we try to put on an act of paying close attention to the speaker, we might come across as domineering or tense. Be wary of this, and, in a relaxed manner, focus on what the speaker is saying.

Tip #3: Do not judge the speaker. Assertive rights call for you to be open-minded and non-judgmental because everyone has a right to his own opinion or view. This assertive right helps you improve your listening skills as well. Being non-judgmental allows you to listen to what the speaker is saying without malice or mockery and respect him or her for it.

Tip #4: Don't interrupt the speaker and impose your solutions(s) in the midst of the conversation. Interrupting while someone is talking sends the wrong signals and is a

typical element of an aggressive communication style. The different messages that a speaker might receive if you interrupt his conversation abruptly include:
- My opinions are more important than yours
- I don't have the energy or the time for your talk
- You are wasting my time
- I don't really care what you think or say

All of us think and speak at different speeds. If you can think and speak faster than your speaker, then it doesn't give you a right to rush her or to stop her midway. Assertiveness calls for you to reduce your speed and align it with that of the speaker so that she and her opinions get the required attention and respect.

Assertive Communication and Handling Criticism

One of the most challenging elements of assertive communication is mastering the art of handling criticism. Here are some tips to help you manage this aspect of assertive communication, depending on the value of the criticism:

Criticism is constructive – Only true well-wishers will take the pains of giving you constructive criticism, facilitating your self-improvement. Therefore, when you know the criticism makes sense and is constructive, accept it wholeheartedly, thank the person, and work on it.

For example, your boss, whom you know has your interests in his heart, finds fault with a presentation that you believed was a great one. Don't get angry with him. Listen to his words attentively, make the necessary changes, and put away the lesson learned for future use.

Criticism is a result of a genuine mistake – If you have made a genuine mistake and someone has found fault with it, don't hesitate to humbly accept your error. Mistakes don't make you a weak or useless person. In fact, accepting your mistake is a sign of courage.

It doesn't matter who has pointed out the mistake. For example, if your subordinate points out an error in your presentation, take it sportingly, thank the person for being so attentive to your presentation, and make the necessary rectifications.

Criticism is unfounded and has no value – One of the best ways to handle negative and valueless criticism is to ignore it completely. However, many times, the criticizer can be nasty enough to say negative things repeatedly. In such circumstances, make sure you tell the person you don't appreciate his or her behavior at all.

Here are some examples of great people who did not let criticism get in the way of their assertiveness:

Mark Twain - One of the most popular humorists of all times, Mark Twain was heavily criticized for his works. Many critics called his novels vulgar and insensitive. In fact, his most famous work, *The Adventures of Huckleberry Finn*, was criticized as being very un-

American. Today, this book is part of many school's academic curricula.

Charles Darwin – It was not easy for this famous scientist to propose his evolution theory based on survival of the fittest. He faced a lot of criticism from religious believers, and the controversy continues today despite having multiple research studies backing his theory.

Final Wrap-Up Practice Tips for Assertiveness

- Remember, you are as valuable as the people around you
- Before you say anything, ask yourself whether it is fair, respectful, and just
- Don't hesitate or be ashamed to voice your desires, needs, and opinions
- Practice emotion management to help you remain calm and composed in any conversation
- Keep your heart and mind open. Remember that, just because you like or dislike something, everyone shouldn't have to follow your preferences.
- Compliment people openly and heartily
- Take criticism in the right spirit

Chapter 7:
Tools to Build Assertiveness

One of the most important elements that reflect your assertiveness is your body language. The use of postures, gestures, the way you present yourself to people, or even a simple handshake can change your communication style from passive to assertive. For example, if you sit up straight in your chair, with your shoulders thrown back confidently, you automatically come across as assertiveness. Contrarily, if you sit with your shoulders slumped, then you appear passive and weak.

Nonverbal communication, of which body language is a critical component, is an essential element of communication. Suppose, for example, that you are giving directions to the cab driver while sitting in the front seat. Now suppose that, mistakenly, you point to the left and say, "Right." The cab driver will turn left, and not right, because your hand gesture pointing to the left is far more impactful than your verbal "right."

Body language and nonverbal cues are powerful communication tools. When you are at a negotiating table, you can actually make out the team with the advantage merely by watching the way they sit. The way you sit or stand is communicating something to the other party and the way the other party sits or stands also communicates something to you. Body language is, in fact, a universal language that breaks all geographical and cultural barriers.

Interestingly, in the animal kingdom, body language also seems to play an important role. For example, expanding the chest (as can be seen in gorillas and apes) is a form of dominance over other animals. Basically, animals "open up" by expanding their chest or spreading out their arms or wings to reflect dominance and aggression.

This expansive gesture seems to be present in the human species as well. If you watch a winner crossing the finishing line in a race, or see someone hit a home run, you will see them open out their arms to form a V, their heads up, with their shoulders thrown back. This expansion is a reflection of the power they feel when they win.

On the other hand, have you noticed losers? They sit with their arms wrapped around themselves, their shoulders slouched, and their heads down. It is as if these losers don't want to touch anyone during their moment of powerlessness.

In the same way, have you observed the way you stand with your boss? Unwittingly, you will have complemented his or power posture. For example, you will have stood next to your boss with your hands folded in and positioned either at the back or in front while your boss stood with his or her arms on her hips or spread out wide. Your boss' expansive power pose is perfectly complemented by your humbling "turned-inward" posture.

Now, take an example when you have called your subordinate to your office to reprimand him for a costly error. Your pose will have been expansive, and your subordinate's pose will have been humbled. This is true most times when two people at different hierarchy levels stand next to each other. Both of them unwittingly complement each other's power poses.

Therefore, we take on a smaller profile when we are next to someone more powerful than us, and we take on a larger profile when we are next to someone less powerful than us.

Power Poses to Increase Assertiveness

Research studies regarding hormonal levels and assertiveness have made some interesting observations. Assertive people tend to have high levels of testosterone and low levels of cortisol.

Cortisol is a hormone connected to anxiety and stress. Therefore, the lower the level of cortisol, the less the level of anxiety and stress. Testosterone is a hormone directly related to confidence. The higher the level of testosterone, the higher the level of confidence. And this relationship between the two hormones and stress and confidence is seen in both men and women.

Thus, low levels of cortisol and high levels of testosterone enhance confidence, reduce stress and anxiety, and increase assertiveness. Additionally, you will feel more in control of your emotions. Therefore, a balanced amount of cortisol and testosterone can help in improving your assertiveness.

The thing about these two hormones, namely cortisol and testosterone, is that their levels can change rapidly and significantly, depending on the mental, emotional, physical, and environmental cues in and around us. Body language is an important cue that can help manage the levels of these two hormones in our bodies.

One of the most effective poses that help in increasing assertiveness levels is the "Wonder Woman" pose in which you stand erect with your hands on your hips and your shoulders straight and strong. Standing in this pose for a couple of minutes can help increase your confidence considerably.

For example, if you need to give a presentation, you are nervous despite all your preparation, and you want to increase your feeling of confidence, then this is what you do. Before you enter the room where people are waiting for your presentation, take the "Wonder Woman" pose and stand for a couple of minutes. You will feel more confident than before.

Don't worry about the Wonder Woman name. It is known to be equally effective for men and women. So, go ahead and use it whenever you need to. In fact, it might be a great idea to make the Wonder Woman stance a part of your morning routine. After you brush your teeth, refresh yourself, get dressed, and prepare to leave for your office, take a couple of minutes to stand in front of the mirror in the Wonder Woman pose. It could be a wonderful morning booster to your confidence and assertiveness levels.

Visualization techniques for assertiveness - Visualize assertive behaviors as often as you can. Visualization activates the subconscious mind to generate ideas to be more assertive than before. It programs your brain to recognize and collect the necessary resources needed to become more assertive. It motivates you to increase your assertiveness.

Increased self-awareness for assertiveness – The more you know yourself, the more assertive you can be. Get to know yourself better by writing down your strengths and weaknesses. Next, accept yourself the way you are. Forget about things you cannot control. Work on things you can control, and take the driver's seat in your life.

Love yourself – If you don't love yourself, no one else will love you. Loving yourself is a critical element to becoming more assertive. Learn the art of enjoying your own company. Learn to understand and manage your thoughts. Take care of your physical and mental health. Don't hesitate to pamper yourself regularly.

Each one of us is unique, and it is up to us to find out what makes us unique. Feel the power of this uniqueness and love yourself for it. You will be more in control of your life if you love yourself. And with increased control comes increased assertiveness.

Use the tools and techniques mentioned in this chapter to become more assertive in your life and leverage the multiple effects of assertiveness.

Chapter 8: Conclusion

Let us look at the multiple benefits of assertiveness in this final chapter so that you are motivated to reread and redo the questionnaires and exercises in this book and build your assertiveness.

Assertive People are Winners and Learners
Assertive people stand up for their rights and are not scared to fail. They simply use their failures to enhance their learning. Therefore, assertive people are either winners or learners. They are never losers.

Assertive People are Loved by All
Assertive people don't use aggression to say what they want to say. Moreover, they stand up for other people's rights as well. They look upon everyone with respect and dignity. Therefore, assertive people are well-loved.

Assertive People are Amazing Communicators
Assertive people learn the art of great communication, including the use of nonverbal cues. They also understand why assertive communication is the best form of

communication. They are aware of their present levels of assertiveness, they know their weaknesses, and they are open-minded to learn and rectify their problems. With the backing of all this knowledge, assertive people become excellent communicators.

Assertive People Tend to have Healthy, Happy Relationships

Excellent communication skills, fantastic ability to voice their own opinions and views without violating the rights of others, and a noble intention to respect and value other people's opinions and views empower assertive people to have healthy, happy relationships that are free from negativities of all kinds. They behave responsibly, handle pressure situations maturely, without being overwhelmed, have no problems in accepting their own mistakes, and are in control of their lives. With all these wonderful traits, assertive people attract a lot of people into their lives and build long-lasting, happy relationships.

Assertive People have High Self-Esteem and Confidence

Assertiveness, confidence, and self-esteem are interminably intertwined, and when one is affected, the other two elements also are impacted in the same way. For example, if you become more assertive than before by practicing and implementing the tips and suggestions in this book, your level of self-esteem and confidence will also see an increase.

Additionally, if you want more detailed information, along with tips and suggestions on self-esteem and confidence, you can choose to buy these books by the same author:

Self-Esteem for Men and *Confidence for Men*.

Assertive People Know the Power of Emotions

Assertive people are highly self-aware which, in turn, means they know and understand their emotions profoundly and thoroughly. They have learned the art of managing their emotions maturely and prudently, empowering them to handle even stressful situations well.

With this basic idea of assertiveness clearly established in your mind, it is wise to reread and redo the exercises in this book, so you understand yourself even better, and you get on the path of increased assertiveness with confidence and high self-esteem.

If you want to know more about what defines confidence, self-esteem, and assertiveness, and how you can go about building these three critical elements into your personality, then do subscribe to our mailing list to receive useful and informative articles regularly.

Part 3: Confidence for Men

3 Secret Hacks to Live Life on Your Terms

By

John Adams

Chapter 1: Introduction – Understanding Confidence

Confidence is the measure of your belief in your own strengths and the identification and acceptance of your weaknesses. A confident man is one who knows the real value of his capabilities and uses them with pride and humbly accepts his drawbacks without being overwhelmed. He feels secure in this knowledge and does not allow his sense of confidence-backed pride to turn to arrogance. A confident man, therefore:

- Has a healthy level of self-worth
- Has a powerful sense of certainty and self-assuredness about his own abilities
- Has faith and trust in himself, and in others
- Is ever-ready to adapt to changing situations
- Is always optimistic and has a clearly-defined set of goals
- Is self-aware and feels motivated to work towards his goals

'A confident man is not one who is always right, but, one who is not afraid of being wrong,' is one the aptest quotes

to define confidence.

Another way to understand confidence is by relating it to low self-esteem and arrogance. Confidence comes from knowing and appreciating your strengths and their real value. Contrarily, arrogance comes because you think you are more valuable than you really are, and low self-esteem comes because you think you are less valuable than you really are.

Confidence is not always about winning. Do you remember the movie *Rocky*? Does the protagonist, Rocky Balboa, win the final fight? No, it ends in a draw. However, people don't really remember the result. They only remember the confidence with which Stallone's character went through all the 15 rounds, never giving up at any time. That is confidence; to continue to battle it out even if you think you might lose.

Also, there is a subtle difference between having confidence and being confident. Having confidence is based on your inner strengths and capabilities while being confident is about appearing confident in front of other people. Typically, people who have confidence present a confident profile to the outside world naturally.

However, there are multiple instances wherein some men appear confident even though they don't feel it inside. This conflict can last for a little while, but, after some time, your lack of confidence within yourself will reflect on the outside as well. Real confidence is quiet and unpretentious. However, when a confident man walks into a room, everyone can feel it.

Why is Confidence Important?

Being confident comes with multiple benefits, and some of them are listed below. However, you must remember that this personality trait is not 'right' or 'wrong.' Don't judge yourself and feel ashamed or guilty if you lack confidence.

First, accept yourself the way you are, and then learn the tricks and tips to build this critical personality trait to leverage its many benefits. The Dalai Lama says, *'A man cannot make peace with the outside world if he hasn't made peace with himself.'*

Look at the life history of James Eugene Carrey, or more famously Jim Carrey. He had a tough childhood when his musician father lost his job, and poverty reared its ugly head in his family. He quit studying at the age of 15 and started working as a janitor to help increase his family's income.

Despite all odds, his passion and confidence in his comic abilities never left him at all. And yet, his debut comedy show was a big flop. But, that didn't deter him. Jim Carrey persisted in his efforts driven by his confidence in himself and his capabilities. His story is a classic example of leveraging the power of confidence to achieve success, despite early setbacks.

Here are some excellent reasons why you should endeavor to build and develop your confidence levels:

You will have a healthy level of self-esteem – When you are confident, you have learned to accept your strengths and weaknesses realistically. You value your capabilities and humbly accept your weaknesses, thereby empowering you to walk with your head held high wherever you go.

For example, suppose you worked hard on a presentation and confidently presented it to your colleagues and seniors in your office. Words of praise for your work will take your confidence and self-esteem levels a few notches up.

Your days will be filled with increased levels of happiness and joy – With increased confidence and self-esteem, you are bound to achieve a lot more success than before. These successes bring a lot of happiness and joy to your life.

For example, if you have not been achieving good sales numbers for two weeks, but have persisted in your efforts consistently and confidently, sales numbers are bound to come sooner rather than later. And when they start coming, the compliments from your boss and the incentives will give you and your family a lot of happiness and joy.

Your capabilities and strengths will get better with increasing confidence – Increased confidence results in improved self-worth and a lot of successes which, in turn, motivate you to upskill yourself and get better at your strengths and capabilities. Each new challenge you encounter will teach you innovative lessons which, in turn, will help build and develop your skills and abilities. Moreover, these challenges can also serve to overcome your weaknesses as you develop your learning.

For example, as you build confidence and get more sales to your credit, you will find ways and means to get better by upskilling yourself through various online courses or attending training sessions or reading books to improve your salesmanship. Success from confident efforts drives you to self-improvement.

You will lose your self-doubting nature – We are all self-doubting naturally because we are uncertain of what to expect, and even more uncertain of whether we can do what we should be doing in a particular situation. As you build confidence and taste the success of your efforts, your self-doubting nature will slowly reduce, and with persistent efforts, will almost disappear. One of the primary reasons for reduced self-doubt is the fact that you realize that confidence comes from accepting failures with equanimity.

Confidence is one of the most attractive qualities in men – Women in particular, and all people in general, find confident men very attractive. Here are some great reasons for that:
- Confident men can handle any situations well. Even in failed situations, you will find confident men giving their most radiant smile reflective of their humble acceptance of defeat, and manfully congratulating the winners.
- Confident men are positive thinkers. No matter how bad a situation might look, confident men will find a positive element in it, and take the forward path from there, and move ahead
- Confident men are powerful leaders who achieve amazing popularity amongst their followers

- Confident men are happy and comfortable being themselves
- Confident men build faith and trust; key elements for people to feel attraction

With so many benefits on offer, it makes sense to work hard to build your level of confidence.

Is Confidence a Genetically Acquired or Learned Skill?

This is a very pertinent question for modern times because, until recently, one of the most popular tenets was that confident men are born, not made. A son of a confident man is confident, and the son of a not-so-confident man is born with little or no confidence. However, nothing can be farther from the truth than this misconception.

For, if this was true, then the son of Abraham Lincoln should have been equally famous as his father. Nelson Mandela's children should have had the same level of confidence that their father had. This does not mean to say that the children of these famous people lacked confidence. However, they were not able to display it at the same level as their fathers did, right?

Biological factors are important to the extent that if you are genetically predisposed to being more confident, building the necessary skills might be easier for you than for someone who is not genetically predisposed in this manner. However, our destinies are not decided by our genes.

Taking the same examples as above, neither Abraham Lincoln's nor Nelson Mandela's father achieved the level of confidence that their sons achieved. Therefore, confidence is a skill that can be learned and mastered and not something that is necessarily acquired genetically.

Building confidence is a matter of developing good habits, creating the right mindset, and working hard towards self-improvement. Here are some more classic examples of people who did all these things, and became super-confident in their lives:

Jeff Bezos – Today, he is one of the richest men on earth. However, he didn't start like that. He simply believed in his vision and capabilities and built an e-commerce industry more than 20 years ago at a time when very few people in the world believed in the power of this market. He continues to innovate his dreams and visions despite achieving amazing success.

Stephen King – This celebrated author was rejected 60 times before he found a publisher who believed in his work. In fact, King wore borrowed clothes for his wedding, and yet nothing stopped him from being confident in his capabilities. He endeavored relentlessly with the support of that belief and achieved amazing success.

Confidence and Assertiveness

Assertive and confidence complement each other. Your confidence comes through when you are assertive, and when you are confident, your assertiveness levels are high.

Yet, there are differences between the two traits. You don't need an external audience to have and feel confident. It's an internal element of your personality that is reflected in your behavior naturally.

However, to be assertive, you need an external audience who form the target of your assertive behavior. There must be some people or person to whom you have to show your assertiveness skills. It is based on perception.

A genuine, deep-rooted reflection of confidence comes out in the form of powerful assertive behavior.

Confidence and Self-Esteem

Self-esteem and confidence are similar traits and are often employed interchangeably. The two traits are connected in the sense that they are directly proportional to each other. And yet, there are differences.

Self-esteem is more or less the same in all aspects of your life. Say, for example, you have high self-esteem in your workplace. Then, it is very likely that you have high self-esteem in your personal life. It is unusual for someone to feel worthy of himself at the office, and unworthy of himself at home, or vice versa. Self-esteem is nothing but the sense of self-worth you possess.

Confidence, on the other hand, can vary across different aspects of your life. For example, you could be a confident professional in your workplace because you have excellent professional skills. However, at home, your confidence level as a father could be quite low because you are uncertain of your parenting skills.

Moreover, confidence is an easier trait to build than self-esteem. Confidence can be easily linked to tangible elements as the skills learned, the outcomes of your efforts, the success achieved, etc. Contrarily, self-esteem is an intangible trait that you must feel within yourself, which is more difficult to understand and build.

Chapter Summary

In this chapter, you learned that confidence is a measure of your self-awareness including your strengths and weaknesses without any underlying arrogance. You also learned the multiple benefits of building confidence, and how it is not as much a genetic skill as it is a learned skill. Anyone can learn and master the art of confidence. You also learned how confidence is linked to assertiveness and self-esteem.

Chapter 2: Understanding Your Current Level of Confidence

Identifying your current level of confidence is the best way to take your confidence-building journey forward. Therefore, this chapter is dedicated to a self-discovery questionnaire and a partner-based self-discovery discussion to help you do just that.

Q1. When my boss gives me a tricky problem to solve, I am confident I can use my professional capabilities to find suitable solutions.
1. Never   2. Sometimes   3. Very often   4. Always

Q2. Using my technical and soft skills, I am confident I can do a great job in my workplace.
1. Never   2. Sometimes   3. Very often   4. Always

Q3. I have always tested my theoretical skills with practical applications.
1. Never   2. Sometimes   3. Very often   4. Always

Q4. I can confidently lead a team to run a challenging project.
1. Never   2. Sometimes   3. Very often   4. Always

Q5. When my team-members come to me with problems, and even though I may not have a solution immediately for them, I am confident to know where to look for the answers.
1. Never   2. Sometimes   3. Very often   4. Always

Q6. I can confidently explain complex theories to my colleagues, team members, and even seniors.
1. Never   2. Sometimes   3. Very often   4. Always

Q7. I am confident of getting my promotions and salary increases based on my performance.
1. Never   2. Sometimes   3. Very often   4. Always

Q8. Would you consider appearing in a TV reality quiz show?
1. Yes   2. I don't know   3. No

Q9. If you are asked to give a long speech about your friend at his wedding, will you accept the task?
1. Yes   2. I don't know   3. No

Q10. Do you believe you are basically a positive individual?

1. Yes   2. I don't know   3. No

Q11. If you were given a choice and you had the necessary skills, would you pilot a plane with over 100 passengers traveling in it?
1. Yes   2. I don't know   3. No

Q12. Would you like to meet high profile and famous people on a one-to-one basis and ask them questions?
1. Yes   2. I am not interested   3. No

Q13. Have you had disagreements with your boss?
1. Yes, Many times   2. A couple of times   3. No, not at all

Q14. Are you comfortable being in front of your friends in swimming trunks?
1. Yes   2. Only with certain people   3. No

Q15. If you were caught by a traffic warden and charged a penalty for an offense, would you contradict him if you believed you were not wrong?
1. Yes   2. I don't know   3. No

Q16. Do you believe in the adage, 'Attack is the best form of defense?'
1. Yes   2. Only sometimes   3. No

Q17. Are you comfortable driving in bad and chaotic traffic?
1. Yes   2. I don't know   3. No

Q18. Are you confident while crossing the road?
1. Yes   2. Not on certain roads   3. No

Q19. If there was a warning of a storm, would you still take the ferry?
1. Yes   2. For an emergency only   3. No

Q20. Do you recall an incident in your life which in retrospect makes you feel you were ruthless?
1. Yes, many   2. Just 1-2   3. No

Q21. Are you impressed by powerful people?
1. Yes   2. No   3. Not often

Q22. Are you someone who ignores warning signs?
1. Yes   2. For an emergency only   3. No

Q23. If you were to choose between two projects, and one was clearly more difficult than the other, would you opt for the difficult one?
1. Yes   2. I don't know   3. No

Q24. Do you believe your intelligence level is above the average person's?
1. Yes   2. I don't know   3. No

Q25. Would you act in a play?
1. Yes   2. I don't know   3. No

Q26. Would you like to train to become a rally car driver?
1. Yes   2. I don't know   3. No

Q27. Would you participate in a dare with your friends to walk through a cemetery in the dead of night?
1. Yes   2. I don't know   3. No

Q28. Are you confident of flying in a small twin-prop engine airplane?
1. Yes   2. I don't know   3. No

Q29. Would you like to stand for election?
1. Yes   2. I don't know   3. No

Q30. Would you walk on a tightrope in a game of dare?
1. Yes   2. I don't know   3. No

Q31. If you are alone at home, and you hear a sound in the kitchen at night, would you get up to go check?
1. Yes   2. I don't know   3. No

Q32. Do you think you are better than most people in your professional and personal social circles?
1. Yes   2. I don't know   3. No

Q33. Do other people's opinions worry or bother you?
1. Yes   2. Sometimes, if the person is someone I care about   3. No

Q34. Are you excessively sensitive to criticism?
1. Yes   2. Sometimes, if the criticizer is my rival   3. No

Q35. Do you feel nervous in front of your boss and those people whose opinions you value?
1. Yes   2. Sometimes, if the outcome is dependent on their opinions   3. No

Q36. Do you think positively about yourself?
1. Always   2. Quite often   3. Rarely   4. Never

Q37. When you are talking to people, do you feel comfortable maintaining eye contact?
1. Always   2. Quite often   3. Rarely   4. Never

Q38. Do you get nervous if you have to speak in front of strangers?
1. Yes   2. I don't know, haven't got an opportunity   3. No

Q39. Do you get nervous if you have to speak in front of family and friends, like at a friend's wedding or a family function?
1. Yes   2. I don't know, I have never been asked to   3. No

Q40. Are you happy with the way you are as a person?
1. Yes   2. Not really, I could have been better   3. No, not at all

Q41. Do you always need external validation to feel good about yourself?
1. Yes   2. I don't know   3. No

Confidence-Gauging Exercise with a Partner
Taking the help of a confidante is another excellent way to arrive at your present levels of confidence. In fact, you and your friend can use this exercise for self-discovery: one helping the other. Now, both imagine a situation which calls for a deep level of confidence.

For example, you can think of giving an impromptu speech at your friend's wedding. Now, both complete this questionnaire based on that imagined situation. For the time being, leave the space for 'friend's comment' blank.

Q1. What do you think will be your emotions? Will it be fear, confidence, or something else?

_____
_____
_____
_____
_____
_____

Friend's comments

_____
_____
_____
_____
_____
_____

Q2. How do you think you will manage your feelings at such a time?

_____
_____
_____
_____
_____

Friend's comments

_____
_____

Q3. What will be your level of preparedness? Will such an impromptu demand on you excite you or drive you into a panic mode?

Friend's comments

Q4. Suppose the audience consisted of only very close family and friends, would your answers be different?

Friend's comments

_____
_____
_____
_____
_____
_____

When both of you have finished the exercise, exchange your notes with your friend. Now, read each other's notes, and make comments in the space for 'friend's comments.' Do you agree with your friend's comments on himself for each of the questions? Has he left out some aspect of his personality which could help you in the situation? Are your views very different from what he believes in himself? Let your friend do the same for you.

This exercise will let you know if what you believe about yourself is what comes across to other people too. For example, suppose your answer to Q1 was, 'I would feel scared and nervous,' and your friend said, 'Not at all, you are a confident person, and you will handle this situation perfectly.'

This means you come across as far more confident than you or, alternatively, you don't believe in your own capabilities as much as others do. This means you are not really self-aware, and your outside profile does not reflect your true inner self. In such conflicting circumstances, ask yourself some more questions to improve self-awareness:

Am I underestimating or overestimating my skills?

Why do I see myself differently from the way others see me?

With the results of these two answers, you will have a reasonably good idea of your current level of confidence, and you can start your development journey from there.

Chapter 3: How to Start Being Confident

The best place to start your journey of building confidence is to make the decision, "I am confident today, and I will be confident every day from now." The decision to change should come first. The other steps will follow naturally. Robert Colliers, one of the most popular writers of self-help books in the 20th century said, *'Take the first step, and your mind will mobilize all its forces to your aid. But the first essential is that you begin. Once the battle is startled, all that is within and without you will come to your assistance.'*

On that note, let us look at two important elements to build your confidence. They are:
• Growth mindset
• Learning and practicing new skills until you master them

Growth Mindset

So, you have made the decision to start being confident

from this moment, and you have taken the first, perhaps most difficult, step. Yet, the path of confidence-building is full of obstacles and challenges, and it is easy to give up on your efforts.

Your confidence level will keep fluctuating depending on multiple factors including your moods, external circumstances, health, and many more reasons. It is imperative that you develop a growth mindset to overcome these challenges and continue relentlessly on your confidence-building journey.

So, what is a growth mindset? Carol S. Dweck, a world-famous psychology professor and researcher, is credited with coining two terms associated with mindset, namely growth mindset and fixed mindset. A man with a fixed mindset believes that his capabilities, his beliefs, his mistakes, the view of the outside world towards himself, and everything else in his life is fixed. Such a man believes that changes, especially growth, are not possible.

If, for example, Bill Gates had had his mindset, then he would have given up after his initial business attempt to create meaningful reports for roadways engineers using raw data failed. Luckily for the world, Bill Gates had a growth mindset. He believed that capabilities, beliefs, mistakes, and everything else in the world are not cast in stone. Anyone with commitment to hard work and persistent efforts and a willingness to learn and grow can overcome challenges and become successful. Today, his success, thanks to his growth mindset, is there for the world to see and try to emulate.

Fixed Mindset Triggers and How to Avoid Them

So, how do you develop a growth mindset to learn new skills and achieve confidence? The first step is to avoid the traps and triggers of a fixed mindset. Along with each of the triggers mentioned, there are growth mindset thoughts and options given for your benefit.

Fixed mindset thought trigger #1 – I cannot develop and build confidence because I am already low on confidence. A growth mindset thinker will, instead, say to himself, "Yes, I am low on confidence right now. However, let me find ways and means to bring it up to scale. Whose help can I take? Are there self-help books available? Can I find a role model whom I can emulate to build confidence? I am certain that if I put in the right kind of efforts to seek help, I can easily develop my confidence, and achieve success."

Fixed mindset thought trigger #2 – I am worried about how I will be perceived by others. Contrary to being obsessed by how others perceive him, a 'growth mindset' man will think like this, "I am unique, and I will show my authentic self to people. It does not matter how I am seen as long as I live my life on my terms."

When you have thought, nothing can stop you from building confidence. You accept and love yourself the way you are. What others think of you should not stop you from doing what you want. Lao Tzu said, *"If you begin to care about what others think of you, you will always remain their prisoner."*

The obsession for 'being perceived right' not only prevents you from achieving your goals but can also drive you insane. Be wary of this important trigger and avoid it completely. Be proud of who you are because as Dr. Seuss said, *"Be who you are, and say what you want to say because those who mind don't matter, and those who matter don't mind."*

Fixed mindset thought trigger #3 – I don't want to try this because what if I fail? Growth mindset thoughts will run something like this: "I have no problem if I fail because if I didn't try, how will I know if I can do it?" Success is almost impossible with encountering failures.

It could be multiple failures like those faced by Thomas Edison (and he said of his 10,000 failures, *"I have not failed 10,000 times. I have only found 10,000 ways how not to do it"*) or it could be one epic failure that stands out like a sore thumb in your life. Failures are the biggest teachers and being scared and running away from them is not just futile but a big deterrent to success and happiness. The only way you can avoid failure is by doing nothing, saying, and being nothing, and that is definitely not living!

Here are some excellent reasons for you to treat failures and mistakes as learning and growing opportunities instead of trying to run away from them:

Mistakes drive our learning – Yes, making mistakes hurt, at least initially. But after that, your brain goes into overdrive and wants to understand what went wrong and find ways and means to correct them. The pain from the mistakes facilitates improved learning because we absorb information much better in this situation than when we are comfortable without the pain.

Mistakes drive self-compassion – We feel sorry and compassionate towards ourselves when we commit errors. This attitude increases our compassion for other people too. Moreover, multiple research studies have proven that compassionate acceptance of our mistakes drives our determination and enthusiasm to learn and improve our skills.

Mistakes free us from limiting fears and empowers us to take calculated risks – After our mistakes come to light, we lose our fear of them. We are freed from these limiting emotions that deter us from taking calculated risks in new and hitherto unchartered territories, giving us opportunities to improve confidence because success lies on the other side of fear.

Mistakes improve motivation – Hitting a big snag in our lives can wake us up from our reverie of comfort driving us to work hard and refresh our commitments to our goals.

Mistakes keep us grounded and humble – An attitude of arrogance is one of the primary adversaries of success. Mistakes help keep this debilitating attitude at bay by reminding us of our vulnerabilities. Mistakes, thus, keep us grounded and humble, which are key elements for success.

Therefore, it is important to remember that life experiences can only result in learning, or winning and not failing.

Fixed mindset thought trigger #4 – I have tried once, and I have failed. I cannot get this right. Giving up easily is one of the biggest drawbacks of having a fixed mindset. A man empowered with a growth mindset will never give up. He will persist because he believes he is on the right track. Temporary setbacks don't deter men with a growth mindset. You must remember nearly all things worthy on this earth don't come easily. Persistence and patience are vital to obtaining worthy elements in life.

Fixed mindset thought trigger #5 – If I have to try so hard, then I don't have the talent for it. Fixed mindset men believe that talented people need not put in efforts and hard work for success. It should come naturally to them. This is a complete myth, and talent is often overrated.

Growth mindset men, on the contrary, know that a great amount of talent without hard work will get you nothing, whereas the basic aptitude for a skill combined with oodles of hard work and commitment can result in outstanding success.

George O' Dowd, better known by his stage name Boy George, was rejected for his 'lack of talent.' That hardly deterred the man who worked hard at his music skills and was able to set a new hip trend in the world of pop music.

Fixed mindset thought trigger #6 – I will not listen to negative feedback because I don't need it. A fixed mindset person is never ready to accept criticism and take feedback with an intention to use it for self-improvement. He will simply ignore it, or worse still, argue with the person giving the feedback.

On the contrary, a man with growth mindset knows and accepts that feedback and criticisms are critical for self-improvement, and he will take them in the right spirit using the useful ones to get better and discarding the spiteful and useless ones.

Learning and Practicing New Skills Until You Master Them

A crucial reason for low levels of confidence is the lack of or insufficient skills. Therefore, it is important to identify critical skills that add value to your life and bring success and happiness. Once you have identified the list of important skills, you must endeavor to build and practice each of those skills until you become a master at it. Here are some tips to help you build new skills and continue learning new things:

Have a curious attitude – Always be interested in knowing how, why, what, why not, etc. A curious attitude is perfect to increase your knowledge and skills. A curious learner imbibes knowledge quickly and effectively. Look at children and learn from their limitless curiosity.

Improve your versatility – When you are good at

many things or can have meaningful conversations with different groups of people, your confidence level is bound to get a boost as more people will appreciate your knowledge and skills. Don't hesitate to learn new skills at all times.

Chapter Summary

In this chapter, you learned the importance of growth mindset to build confidence. You also learned tips and tricks on how to have a growth mindset and how to practice a new skill until you become a master at it.

Chapter 4: Self-Awareness - Know Your Core Values

What are core values and why are they important in your life? This is the best way to make a list of your core values based on which you will lead your life.

So, what are core values? We value a lot of things and people in our lives. For example, you could value your home, your wife, kids, parents, teachers, your job, your friends, etc. Many of your choices in life are based on the priorities you give to the people and things you value.

For instance, suppose you have to choose between going to work on a weekend to complete an important project with a deadline coming up very soon and taking your kids out on a picnic that you promised last week. Your choice will depend on the value you have given to your kids and your job.

Which is more important in your life? What makes your life worthwhile? Your choices are founded on those priorities. Remember there are no right or wrong answers.

They are a reflection of which values are important to you and how you rank them in your life, that's all. Like Elvis Presley said, *"Values are like fingerprints. Nobody's are the same as anyone else's; but you leave them all over everything you do."*

Core values are qualities or traits that guide and drive your life and life choices. Core values not only help you live a happy life but also give you valid reasons to make the right decisions so that you lead a fulfilling and meaningful life.

Importance of Core Values

Core values give you a sense of purpose – Most of us don't really have a purpose in life. We drift along going where our lives take us, uncertain of where we want to reach. Only when you know what is important in your life can you know what you want from it. Core values help you understand your priorities in life.

Core values help you make the right choices in difficult situations – Core values become our guiding principles in life and help us make the right choice in difficult situations. You can easily align your behavior with your core values. Core values, therefore, are a beacon to show you the path of your life.

Moreover, when you are stuck in a dilemma, and are unsure what you need to do, core values will shed light on the darkness. They will tell you whether you should apologize in a particular situation and back off or stand your ground and fight for your rights. For example, in the example given above, when you had to choose between your kids and office work, your core values will help you decide what comes first in this situation.

Core values help you clear off all kinds of clutter from your life – With your core values in place, you can get rid of all other things that are not aligned to them and clear your life of all kinds of clutter keeping it simple and minimalistic. The modern world consumes your life in so many ways, including social media, television media, print media, internet, and others that can lead to a feeling of claustrophobia. Clearing clutter will give your life a semblance of order.

Core values help you make the right career choice – No career is perfect. Every career has its pros and cons. With the right set of core values to guide you, you can make the right career choice that is aligned with your life goals and missions.

For example, if you value family more than anything else, then you could choose a career that gives you the flexibility of working from home. Contrarily, if you love traveling and adventure, you could choose a job that entails both these elements. Many times, identifying and developing a deep connection with your core values might give you an idea if a promotion is worth it or not!

Core values increase your level of confidence – Core values give your life a sense of certainty and stability which, in turn, helps to build your level of confidence. When you are clear about your needs, it doesn't matter what people want. You will confidently work to fulfill your needs.

Characteristics of Core Values

There are over 400 core values you can choose from. Before we go into a self-exploratory exercise on how to identify your personal core values, let us understand the basic characteristics that define core values.

Core values should be implementable in all conditions of your life – For example, honesty is a core value that you can implement no matter what condition you are in. You could be young, old, or in a wheelchair, bedridden, or anywhere else or any other state. You can still remain honest.

However, if you choose physical fitness, then this is not possible in all conditions of your life. In your bedridden state or on a wheelchair, maintaining physical fitness can be quite a challenge.

Practicing your core values should not depend on any external factor – If you choose popularity as one of your core values, then you need other people to like you in order to be popular. Therefore, this cannot be a core value in your life. But, courage or discipline does not depend on any other factor to help you implement and follow in your life.

Self-Assessment Exercise to Arrive at Your Core Values
One way of creating core values that you think worthwhile is to look at the list of over 400 available on the internet and choose from there. Some of them include adventure, freedom, ambition, family, integrity, courage, respect, fun, money, health, and many, many more.

However, the best way to make your core values list is to examine your life and your experiences and see what helped you grow and become a better individual, and what prevented you from growing and getting better. From these experiences, you can cull your list of personal core values.

Before you start this exercise, grab a pen and a notebook, and a few sticky notes to pen down your thoughts as they come to you. And give yourself at least an hour to complete this exercise satisfactorily. Now, write down answers to these questions:

Step 1: What were the best experiences in your life? Choose between 3-5 experiences that you believe made you the happiest and gave you a deep sense of satisfaction. Write answers to the following questions for each of those experiences:

Describe the experience in detail including when it happened, how old you were, what happened, and other factual details.

_____
_____
_____
_____
_____
_____
_____

Write the most significant emotions you felt at that time. Strangely, you will notice that such powerful experiences bring back that rush of emotion, even now. Use that to make detailed notes.

_____
_____
_____
_____
_____
_____

What were the core values that were being played out in those experiences? If the experience took place many years ago, maybe when you were a child, you may not have understood what core values were at that time. Now, however, when you recall those past experiences, you will be able to clearly label the core values that stood out during the event.

_____
_____
_____
_____
_____
_____

Step 2: In the same way, recall and write down the worst experiences of your life, and answer the following questions:

Describe the experience in detail including when it happened, how old you were, what happened, and other factual details.

_____
_____

_____
_____
_____
_____
_____

Write the most significant emotions you felt at that time.
_____
_____
_____
_____
_____
_____
_____

What were the core values that were being stifled out in those experiences?
_____
_____
_____
_____
_____
_____
_____

Step 3: Define your code of conduct. To do this, you have to reflect deeply, and think of those elements in your life that come immediately after your basic survival needs are met. These elements are those that add meaning and joy to your life, and in their absence, you live life like an automaton.

Some examples include:
- Adventure

- Freedom
- Health and vitality
- Learning and growth
- Creativity

Step 4: Collect all the core values you got from the answers to the above questions and combine similar core values together. For instance, you can combine productivity, efficiency, ambition, accomplishment, etc. under career. You can combine generosity, altruism, helpful, doing good to others, etc. under service-oriented.

If it is a long list, then you need to pick the top 5-10 from this list. Keeping less than 5 items in your core values list might not cover all the important tenets of life and keeping more than 10 items might create challenges for you to work with practically.

The last thing you must do is prioritize your core values in order of importance in your life. Although this activity appears simple, it could take a while. How do you rank elements that look equally important? Revisit your best and worst experiences and see if you can recall the intensity of the emotions in each of those cases. The more the intensity, the deeper you felt about that particular core value. Using the data from this exercise, you might be able to rank your core values list in order of importance.

Keep sticky notes of your core values and put them all over so that you read them daily and imbibe them deeply in your psyche.

Chapter Summary

In this chapter, you learned the definition, significance, and characteristic features of core values. Complete the experience-based exercise to arrive at your own core values.

Chapter 5: Setting Goals; Your Mission and Purpose

Your core values are in place, and they are deeply imbibed in your psyche. The next thing to do is set goals for your life. A life mission gives you purpose in life, and when you walk the goal path supported by your core values, you will be able to lead a more fulfilling and meaningful life.

Why is Goal-Setting Important?

"If you want to be happy, set a goal that commands your thoughts, liberates your energy and inspires your hopes," said Andrew Carnegie. Here are some amazing reasons why you must start setting goals today:

Goal-setting helps you achieve faster and effective results – When you have clear goals in place, you can focus on how to achieve them and not waste your time and energy focusing on what you want to achieve. With clear goals, you can work slowly daily and make certain progress towards your goal each day. As you achieve each day's goal, you will find the motivation to work hard for the next day's goal, ensuring you are making daily progress.

Clear goals improve positive attitude – Goals have the power to drive you to achieve them and put you firmly in the driver's seat. Goals are what make your dream tangible targets that can be made into daily, weekly, and monthly goals, giving you the satisfaction of achieving a little at a time. This achievement nurtures positivity in your life.

Goals prevent procrastination – Procrastination is a debilitating habit and is one of the biggest hurdles to advancement and growth. Your sense of focus and purpose is significantly improved with goal-setting, which, in turn, ensures you don't allow yourself to get into a procrastination mode. Moreover, as you break your large and long-term goals into smaller ones achievable over a shorter period, you will find it easy to do what is necessary for each little advancement without procrastinating.

Goals improve time management – Knowing exactly what you want and by when you want it ensures you don't waste time on unproductive work. You will be able to manage your time more effectively than if you didn't have clear-set goals.

Goals prevent you from getting distracted – Goals are your self-imposed boundaries keeping you on your chosen path that is moving towards your purpose. Deep-seated goals ensure your mind is quickly attuned to distractions and gives you a warning signal if you think of straying from your path.

Here is a simple example of the power of goal-setting. Suppose you had a meeting with your boss at 10 in the morning. You know you have a 15-minute walk from the station to your office. You will ensure that you get the earlier train that day and walk briskly from the station, making sure you are focused on the walk and are not distracted by anything including the coffee shop that you usually stop by for your second cup of coffee.

When your mind imbibes the power of a simple goal such as meeting with your boss and keeps you safe from distractions, you can only imagine how much more aware it will be when you have large goals deeply imbibed in your psyche.

Goals facilitate improved decision-making abilities – Every time you have to make a choice or take a decision, all you need to do is ask yourself: "Does this help you get closer to my goals or not?" You can make sensible decisions depending on the answer you get.

For example, if you have a goal of completing the presentation by the end of the day, and your friends call you to watch a game on TV, ask yourself, "What will help you reach my predetermined goal?" Then, you will find it easy to say no to your friends because that choice clearly takes you further away from your daily goal. Therefore, goals help you say NO firmly and assertively.

Self-Discovery Questions for Goal-Setting
Before you set goals based on your core values, you must know what kind of goals you must set. And for that, you

need to be indulge in self-exploratory exercises to understand what you want from your life. Reflect on the following questions and write down your answers:

Q1. What is your definition of a meaningful life? If you think this question is very broad-based, break it up into the following questions:
- What moves you to work hard and drive myself?
- What motivates you?
- What are your desires?
- What are the things you care deeply about?

_____
_____
_____
_____
_____
_____
_____

Q2. What was your position in your life previous to now? What are your past experiences? Write down both good and bad experiences. Using the memories, you can get an idea of where you were before now.

_____
_____
_____
_____
_____
_____
_____

Q3. Where do you stand today? Use the following questions to get insights for this aspect of your self-

discovery process:
- What kind of a person are you?
- What are your capabilities?
- What are your weaknesses?
- What do you love doing?
- What do you hate doing?

Q4. Where do you want to be 10 years from now? The answers to this question will give you an idea of where to begin your goal-setting process. To get a complete understanding of your goals, find answers to the following questions:
- What are the skills and abilities you want to build?
- What are the money and wealth goals I have?
- From a career perspective, what position do you want to reach?
- What kind of future do you envision for your loved ones?

Q5. Here some the specific goal-setting questions. Indulge in a little bit of self-reflection and find answers to them. You might need to do some research too.
- What are the steps you need to take to get there?
- What are the resources you need to get for myself?
- What are the impending obstacles?
- How can you overcome these obstacles?
- Who can help you to achieve your goals? How can you approach them?
- What are the elements that are holding you back?

_____
_____
_____
_____
_____
_____
_____

Once, you have these long-term goals in place, break them into daily, weekly, and monthly goals to keep track of them. Use the following template to help you make notes of your goals and whether you have achieved them.

Daily Goals Worksheet
Before retiring to bed each night, complete this daily goals worksheet:
My goal for tomorrow is:

_____
_____
_____
_____

What steps are needed to ensure these goals are reached?

Weekly Goals Worksheet

Typically, you must complete this either on Sunday night or Monday morning depending on your lifestyle. It would be even better if you could complete it by Saturday night before you set out for your weekend socializing so that you don't forget about it.

My goals for the upcoming week are

What steps are needed to ensure these goals are reached?

Like this, you can make monthly goals and yearly goals as well. Here are some classic examples of goals for men:

- ***Health goals:*** I want to lose 20 pounds by the end of the half-year. To achieve this, I will exercise every day, keep track of my food intake, and get myself a good health insurance.
- ***Creative goals:*** I want to pursue my hobby of playing the guitar. To achieve this, I will join classes from this week, and allocate 30 minutes each day towards my practice.
- ***Spiritual goals:*** I will meditate 15 minutes every day starting from today. I will volunteer at the orphanage or old age home every second Sunday of the month
- ***Financial goals:*** I will start saving $500 every month starting from this month. That will ensure I have $6000 of my own money at the end of the year.

Chapter Summary

In this chapter, you learned the importance of goal-setting, and how to match your goals to your core values. This chapter also includes worksheet templates you can use for your goal-setting process.

Chapter 6: Tips and Tricks to Build Confidence - Part I

This and the next chapters are dedicated to giving you tips and tricks to build confidence.

Building Confidence through Visualizations

Visualization is nothing but daydreaming with a sense of purpose. Richard Bach, the famous author said, *"To bring anything into your life, imagine that it's already there."* Visualization is a powerful tool to help crystallize dreams.

Arnold Schwarzenegger used visualization techniques to realize his body-building dreams. His role model was Reg Park, the famous English bodybuilder of the 1950s. Arnold said that he kept visualizing himself with his role model's body and was motivated to commit himself wholeheartedly to achieve his dream.

How does visualization help us realize our dreams? Multiple research studies have shown that when we imagine a scene in our heads, the primal parts of our brain behave like the imaginary scene was really happening. Imaginations are known to affect our central nervous system directly.

Therefore, you experience an inexplicable feeling of dread even when you merely imagine yourself facing dangers. Similarly, when you imagine yourself sitting on a beach enjoying the beautiful blue sea, you feel a sense of peace and calmness. Here are some excellent benefits of using visualization techniques to build confidence:

- It activates your subconscious mind to generate excellent ideas to help you achieve your goals
- It programs your brain to quickly and effectively identify and attract resources that can help you achieve your goals.
- The repeated practice of visualization technique helps activate the law of attraction drawing people, resources, and other useful elements into your life.
- It enhances motivation and confidence

Thus, it makes sense to use visualization to increase your confidence levels. Here is an example you can use as a template for visualization exercises in your life:

Visualization Exercise: Suppose you need to ask your boss for a raise. You are feeling nervous and your confidence levels are low, and yet, you know you deserve the raise. Here is what you can do to get rid of nervousness and build your confidence levels before approaching your boss:

First, prepare what you will say to your boss starting from the greeting stage. Make sure you have substantial data about your achievements and solid reasons why you

believe you deserve the raise. Practice your speech well.
- Find a quiet place where you will not be disturbed. Sit comfortably.
- Close your eyes and take a deep breath.
- Visualize yourself walking confidently to your boss' cabin and knocking on the door.
- Imagine him giving you permission to enter
- Visualize greeting him confidently and tell him that you have something important to discuss.
- Visualize your boss offering you a seat.
- Imagine giving the prepared speech calmly and confidently. Rehearse the speech in your visualization exercise.
- Visualize your boss giving you a smile and telling you that he agrees with your views.

Keep imagining this happy sequence. Visualizing does not guarantee the exact same outcome in reality. However, repeated visualization helps to eliminate nervousness which, in turn, builds confidence. It is like rehearsing for a play. The more skilled you become, the more confident you get.

Confidence Building through Affirmations

Affirmations are not just mantras to make you feel better. They have the power to make your dreams come true. Affirmations encourage you to lead a more fulfilling and meaningful life than before. Here are some excellent benefits of using affirmations to build confidence:
- Daily affirmations enhance your ability to become

acutely aware of your thoughts and emotions thereby preventing negativities from creeping in.
- Your thoughts and actions synchronize with each other, resulting in increased efficiency and productivity.
- Affirmations draw things that you desire into your life, and bring in a lot of divine blessings.
- Affirmations keep you aware of and grateful for the seemingly small elements in your life that bring you a lot of joy and happiness. In the mad rush of the modern world, we tend to forget little things that truly matter in our lives including the joy of loved ones, the comforts of a beautiful home, a healthy body, and more.
- Affirmations help you remain positive which, in turn, builds confidence.
- Affirmations keep your focused and motivated.

Here are some excellent confidence-building affirmations you can try daily. In fact, start your day with an affirmation, and end your day with another.
- I am fearless.
- I am mindful, calm, and confident.
- I am always trying to get better. But, today, I am happy with what I have.
- I am a positive person, and I believe in my capabilities.
- I am compassionate with others and with myself.
- I have the confidence to overcome all obstacles.
- I love to meet new people and have conversations with them.
- I am wise, strong, and powerful.
- I am complete by myself.
- I am my best friend and my best source of

motivation.
- Life is beautiful, and I am happy to live it to the fullest.
- Challenges help me grow and learn.
- I am a positive man, and therefore, attract only positive people to myself.
- I am unique, and that's what gives me a strong individuality.
- I make a difference even if I simply turn out each day and give my best.
- Each day, I am becoming better than yesterday.
- I deserve my desires because I have the capabilities to achieve them, and I work hard for them.
- I am focused on solutions. Obstacles do not deter me.
- I am confident of successfully completing my responsibilities and tasks.
- I love myself, and I look for the best in every situation.
- I am very happy to receive compliments because I know I deserve them.
- I feel grateful for my life and all its offerings.
- Everything is possible provided I am willing to work hard and commit myself.
- I am an open person and I love to look at things in new perspectives.
- I am intelligent and talented.
- I am confident and enthusiastic.
- I am not afraid of making mistakes.

Whenever you feel your confidence ebbing, get away to a quiet and undisturbed place, and repeat your favorite affirmations for a couple of minutes. The problem you had will not go away with affirmations. But your will and resolve to overcome the problem will be multiplied.

Challenge Yourself Continuously

Challenging yourself continuously is the most effective way for self-improvement. If what you are doing does not challenge you and your capabilities, then you are not growing. You are stagnating, which is the first step to downfall. Staying in your comfort zone is the biggest hurdle to building confidence. The longer you remain in your comfort zone, the more complacent you get. The more complacent you get, the more difficult it is to get out of your comfort zone.

The Lotus Eaters in Greek mythology is a classic example of people who were so complacent in their comfort zone that they died even before they started to live. They forgot everything else except to eat the lotus. They stagnated and died on that island. A similar thing can happen to you if you don't get outside of your comfort zone and challenge yourself continually.

Challenging yourself, accomplishing new projects and tasks, doing unfamiliar activities, taking tough decisions, getting physically and mentally uncomfortable, and other such activities are excellent ways of building confidence. Help others as much as you can. However, before helping others, help yourself.

Build your skill sets. Become a master in multiple domains, and you will find yourself becoming increasingly confident with each new skill you acquire. Every time you learn a new skill, you are challenging yourself, and raising the bar for self-improvement.

Here are some excellent tips to continuously challenge yourself:

Do something you dislike – If you hate washing dishes, and your wife is constantly nagging you to do it, then give in to her nagging, and wash dishes without complaining for a week. Promise yourself this, and each time you want to complain, remember the promise, and consciously stop yourself from whining. Instead, get off the couch and wash the dishes. It is possible that your wife is going to be super surprised and will want to return the favor in a way you like.

Another example is if you don't like talking to a particular colleague, make an effort for a week to start the conversation with him or her. If you hate to dance, learn dancing. If you don't like to cook, make an effort to help your wife in the kitchen.

What is your biggest fear? Live with it for a week – For example, if you are afraid of change, begin to tackle this fear by making changes in your daily routine. Instead of having breakfast after your bath, have a bath after you eat simply because it is different from your normal routine and will result in making you uncomfortable.

If you are scared to speak in public, use every opportunity you get to speak in front of other people. If you are scared of embarrassment, then try singing loudly or doing something embarrassing in front of people whom you trust. Slowly, the fear will fade. If you are scared of a particular relative, invite him home for a week.

What is your biggest love? Stay away from it for a week – If you love your daily Netflix movie indulgence, then uninstall the app for a week. If you love Facebook or any other social media platform, uninstall the apps for a while.

Do things differently - If you are a left-handed person, then eat with your right hand, and vice versa. If you brush your teeth with your right hand, use your left hand for a week.

Basically, don't allow yourself to feel comfortable. The less comfortable you feel, the more alert you will be. You will be able to garner a lot of skills with this attitude, resulting in improved confidence.

Journals for Confidence Building

Stephen R. Covey, the author of the best-selling book, "The Seven Habits of Highly Effective People," and many others, said, "Keeping a personal journal a daily in-depth analysis and evaluation of your experiences is a high-leverage activity that increases self-awareness and enhances all the endowments and the synergy among them." There are multiple benefits to maintaining a journal. Some of them include:

• Journaling helps you have clarity on your goals and their statuses.
• Journaling helps in daily recovery as you write

down and let go of all the emotions of the day.
- Journaling helps you weed out inconsistencies in your life.
- Journaling enhances the power of your learning as you make notes of your daily experiences.
- Journaling helps you keep track of your daily, weekly, and monthly goals. This activity gives you opportunities to tweak and make changes to your goals whenever.
- Journaling improves your sense of gratitude

All these benefits directly impact your confidence levels. In addition to making journal entries of your daily experience, you can make write down positive thoughts to counter confidence-depleting negative thoughts. Here are a few examples for you:

Negative thought: 'I cannot do this.'
- ***Journal prompt #1:*** Make a list of all your achievements right from your school days until last week.
- ***Journal prompt #2:*** Write down an experience which entailed a similar situation. You thought you couldn't do it, but you not only completed it but also did it well.
- ***Journal prompt #3:*** What is the most courageous thing you ever did?

Negative thought: 'I have poor knowledge.'
- ***Journal prompt #1:*** Make a list of subjects where you have excellent knowledge levels. Include the number of hours you have spent learning that topic. What kinds of training you have had? How you have used that knowledge successfully?

- *Journal prompt #2:* Make a list of the things you will do to increase your currently poor knowledge levels

Negative thought: 'I think I am very ugly or very fat, and I don't like my looks.'

- *Journal prompt #1:* What are you happy about in your body? List at least two things.
- *Journal prompt #2:* Make a list of things you are grateful for in your physical body. It can be something as simple as your flexibility, the way your fingers are shaped, your smile, or anything else
- *Journal prompt #3:* What are the compliments you have received for your looks?

Negative thought: 'I lack good qualities.'

- *Journal prompt #1:* List the things you are grateful in yourself.
- *Journal prompt #2:* List the top two compliments you have got from people.
- *Journal prompt #3:* What does your best friend think of you?
- *Journal prompt #4:* What do you like about yourself?

Negative thought: 'I will definitely fail, therefore I will not try it.'

Journal prompt #1: List the good things that will happen if you DON'T fail.

Journal prompt #2: Make a note of the worst-case scenario. Now, find ways to means manage the situation even if this was to happen.

Chapter Summary

In this chapter, you learned three different ways to build

confidence including using visualization techniques, affirmations, challenging yourself, and journaling.

Chapter 7: Tips and Tricks to Build Confidence - Part II

Avoid Perfectionism

Perfection is only an excuse for self-criticism. Even gold in its perfect form can never be made into beautiful jewelry. It needs a bit of imperfection in the form of copper to create stunning artwork. You are motivated by striving for excellence whereas you feel demoralized if you strive for perfection. Leo Tolstoy said, *"If you look for perfection, you will never find contentment and happiness."*

Trying your best to do a job well is a healthy attitude to have. Being obsessed with perfectionism is a dangerously unhealthy trait to have. Perfectionism is one of the primary obstacles of confidence building. An obsessive perfectionist is plagued by these negative and debilitating thoughts and emotions:

- I don't like the way I am at present.
- I never seem to be satisfied with anything.
- I see the entire world and all it's happening in black and white. I cannot forgive myself or anybody else for being grey which is the color of the realistic world.

- I think if I achieve perfection I will be at peace.
- I have to constantly overachieve to feel even a small amount of satisfaction.
- If I don't get exactly what I set my mind to, I complain and whine.
- Efforts and intentions are never enough. I should see tangible and flawless results.

What happens if you try to be a perfectionist? Here are some challenges that will negatively impact your daily life, making it miserable and unlivable:

You are always anxious and tired – In your efforts to overachieve and better yourself each time, you will be in a constant state of high-alert, leading to excessive stress, fatigue, and anxiety. Also, the incremental energy needed to take a job well done to a 'perfect' level is significantly larger than what you used to reach the level of excellence. The incremental benefit is not worthy of this effort. Thus, perfection uses up excessive energy needlessly.

Unhappy relationships - Driven by the stress of your unreasonable expectations, people who are in a relationship with you will always feel anxious and worried. This kind of worry can easily ruin a relationship sooner rather than later. You are constantly finding fault with your wife or partner which can drive her crazy, and she is bound to walk out.

Similarly, your unreasonable expectations from your

children can make them either fear you or hate you as a father. Relationships from all sides are bound to suffer if you are obsessed with perfection.

You will always feel guilty or ashamed of yourself – Perfectionists look at the outside world as a reflection of their inner self. So, if you are a perfectionist and you see a mess, clutter, or disorganization around you, you transfer that mess and clutter into yourself. This outlook fills them with shame and guilt for not doing your job well which is not the true picture. Therefore, you are always plagued by a sense of guilt and shame.

Instead of trying to be Mr. Perfect, make sure you have given your best at everything, and leave it at that. Here are some tips to help you overcome the obsession over perfection:

Know that perfectionism is a myth – Perfectionism, like all things in this world, is relative. What is perfect for you could be just be good enough for someone else, and vice versa. Also, in your own life, the concept of perfectionism is different for different aspects. For example, at your work, you could expect perfection from your subordinates whereas at home you could choose to be slack with your kids. Therefore, accept that perfectionism is only in your head, and is not possible in real life.

Learn to accept being good enough – Accepting good enough is not slacking off from doing your best. It only means to give up obsessing over perfection. We can find a good-enough level for all the work we do. Don't waste precious time and energy resources to following up with perfectionism.

For example, if your office presentation for monthly sales has come out accurately and up to expectations, then don't feel the unnecessary pressure of being the expert mathematician and try to get the numbers perfectly right up to the 6th decimal place! Let it be and go with the accurate figures.

Accept that human beings are imperfect and will make mistakes – Human beings are imperfect, and our world is full of flaws. Things are bound to go wrong sometimes. Accept mistakes as learning opportunities and move on.

And finally, the people who matter in your life will never reject you for human imperfections. In fact, your loved ones will love you more for your mistakes because it makes you more human and endearing. Of course, these tips to avoid perfectionism does not mean you don't try to do your best. It is only to help you overcome your obsession with perfectionism.

Love Yourself

The relationship you share with yourself sets the tone for every other relationship you have or will have with others. Oscar Wilde said, *'To love oneself is the beginning of a lifelong, never-ending romance.'*

Loving yourself does not mean being narcissistic or self-centered. It only means you identify, respect, and accept yourself the way you are and for what you are. Self-love is a quality that gives us control over our own lives while teaching us to be compassionate towards everyone starting from ourselves. Here are some great benefits of loving ourselves:

- We are free from greed, anger, and resentment because we wholeheartedly accept ourselves the way we are, and therefore, we don't find ourselves wanting anything.
- We are free from the worry about how others perceive us because it doesn't matter to us anymore.
- We are free from having to maintain a façade for the sake of the outside world. Our behavior becomes authentic.
- We love our own company and don't feel lonely when we are alone.
- We are free from fear because we know we are always there for ourselves.
- We take control of our lives as we realize that only we are responsible for bringing joy and happiness for ourselves.

How can we love ourselves? Here are some tips for you:

List all the good things in your life – The list of good things in your life helps you perceive your life positively. You focus on the elements that make you happy. This attitude makes you realize the abundance of joy in your life. When you realize this abundance, you learn yourself and your life more.

Surround yourself with people who love you – While self-love is very important, sometimes we need people to reiterate their love for us to feel good and happy. Create a loving social circle around yourself filled with people who care for and like you and will not hesitate to say so when you are down and depressed.

Maintain a clean and hygienic lifestyle – Remove physical, mental, and emotional clutter from your life. Maintain a clean, negativity-free, and clutter-free lifestyle. This attitude will give you a sense of freedom, happiness, and lightness that is in stark contrast to the feeling of heaviness that comes with a cluttered, negativity-filled, and disorganized lifestyle.

Use these self-love practices daily:

- Start your day with a self-love affirmation.
- Respect and love your body.
- Don't take your thoughts seriously. Many of them, especially the negative ones, come only to scare and confuse you.
- You are unique. Therefore, don't ever compare yourself with anyone else.
- Be proud of your achievements.
- Keep away from all kinds of toxicity from your life. Avoid people who demoralize you, think you are useless, mistreat you, etc.

Have a Positive Attitude

Confucius said, 'To put the world right in order, we must first put the nation in order; to put the nation in order, we must first put the family in order; to put the family in order, we must first cultivate our personal life; we must first set our hearts right.'

Keep a positive attitude if you want to build confidence. The more positive you are, the more positive elements come into your life. Here are some great benefits to having a positive attitude:

Challenges become opportunities – When you see everything in a positive light, then challenges become opportunities for your development, and not obstacles to stifle your growth. When you see opportunities instead of challenges, you will find creative solutions that bring you success. Increased success translates to increased confidence.

Increased motivation – With a positive attitude, you feel motivated to give your best resulting in increased chances of success which, in turn, enhance confidence and self-esteem.

Reduction in stress levels – Negative thoughts and attitudes fill your mind with stress and anxiety. A positive outlook reduces the level of stress because you choose to focus on the good things. Therefore, you can use your energy to do productive work instead of using it to manage undue stress and anxiety.

Here are some tips to build a positive attitude:

Live in the moment – Worrying about the past and future leads to unnecessary negativity. You are wasting your time and energy regretting the past and thinking about an uncertain future. Living in the moment empowers you to experience life fully and fills you with a positive feeling.

Use positive words to describe yourself and your life – Our choice of words have a powerful impact on our lives. If we use negative words to describe our life, then that is how you perceive it. For example, if you say, 'My job is boring, mundane, and busy,' then that is how your job is. However, if you say, 'My job is exciting, unique, and different,' then your job becomes that. The situation does not impact your life as much as your response to it. Therefore, always use positive words to bring positivity into your life.

Replace 'have' with 'get' – Here are some examples:
- 'I have to pay rent' must become 'I get to pay rent.'
- *'I have to go to work'* must become *'I get to go to work.'*

The sentence with the 'have' sounds obligatory whereas the sentence with 'get' sounds like an opportunity. One simple change of word results in perceiving things positively.

Surround yourself with positive people always, and be conscious of your every action, thought, and response so that you can choose to be positive rather than negative. Surround yourself with confident people. Don't be jealous of their confidence. Simply learn from them and imbibe their qualities into your life.

Chapter Summary

In this chapter, you learned how to build confidence by avoid perfectionism, loving and respecting yourself, and having a positive attitude.

Chapter 8: Conclusion

The main takeaways from this book include:

- Building confidence begins with your simple decision to wake up each morning and promise yourself that you will be confident today.
- Understand your current level of confidence so that you know what you need to do next to get better at it.
- Create a growth mindset and learn to master skills you are not good at.
- Create your core values based on your life experiences. Understanding your core values helps you relate openly and honestly with your strengths and weaknesses.
- Use your core values and create goals for your life. The absence of clear goals and a life purpose will constantly throw you into a confused state of mind. With clearly established goals and life purposes, you are absolutely certain of the life path you need to take to achieve your goals. This sense of certainty boosts your confidence level significantly.
- Knowing and identifying your goals empowers you to live your life on your terms and not be worried about what others think.

- Tips and tricks on how to build confidence in your life.

So, go ahead, and start your confidence building journey today!

Confidence is closely related to assertiveness and self-esteem. When the value of one increases, the value of the other two also goes up in your life. There are two other books by John Adams titled 'Self-Esteem for Men' and 'Assertiveness for Men.' that deal with assertiveness and self-esteem in the same way this book deals with confidence. Read them to get a complete overhaul of your life.

Printed in Great Britain
by Amazon